Project Leadership for the 21st Century

by Martin Crump & Matthew Theobald

Contents

A First Word

This book is about changing the way you look at projects, sharing a completely new way of running them. A way that focuses on people and leadership rather than the nuts and bolts of tasks. That approach was fine in the past, but now, with the rapid changes in the working environment and the technology supporting it, we need a less complex way, a way that values people.

Before the industrial age changed how we lived our lives, people were still able to build great cathedrals, they made tremendous leaps in scientific understanding. From biblical times, there's a great example of project management, in Noah's Ark. Noah was given a crystal clear purpose and detailed specification, with the "how" left up to him. In this post-industrial age, perhaps it is time to return full circle, to emphasise the value of leadership, providing space for the project team to deliver.

As you read, you will learn about the really important stuff of leading a project, a simple three step process to get you from A to Z. You will discover what should be taken care of at each step on your journey. You'll find out about the tools and techniques, along with how to use them, at each step along the way.

You will hear about the way we went about writing this book, follow our journey through the very same three steps, see the results from our use of the tools and techniques talked about.

We hope you enjoy your journey.

Martin and Matthew, July 2011

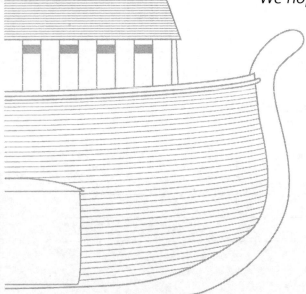

Why Project Leadership?

People who have been involved with projects consistently say they struggle to get to grips with the nuts and bolts of project delivery. Is there a fracture between the theory of project management and the reality of working in a project organisation?

The field of project management is considered by many to be a maturing discipline. There are several professional organisations around the world that have developed detailed methodologies to manage projects along with certification programmes for their use. The number of books written on the subject would fill many, many book shelves, mainly focussing on the technical aspects. There are conferences, webinars, journals, industry interest groups and numerous training courses available for the interested person.

Working with other organisations

More and more, the projects we all work on involve several organisations. There is an accompanying increase in the reliance on external partners (or suppliers) for expertise and knowledge that isn't available within the company initiating the project. In tandem with this changing landscape, there is pressure to "get more out" of suppliers, for lower investment (financial, resource and technical). This is the case for organisations small and large, public and private sector. The need for strong, honest relationships has never been more acute, yet the drive to reduce costs and "manage the supply chain" pushes us towards lowest up front cost solutions and neglects the human element that is vital to any business relationship.

When you're in the thick of it, working across departments and organisations, how often has someone said to you that a document must be completed, but they can't tell you what purpose that document really serves? Do projects feel to rush headlong into "doing something, anything" maybe even taking extreme tactics to avoid thinking and talking about what the project is there to do, and how you could sensibly deliver it? Do you feel a push back from suppliers (or clients) to skip over these "soft" steps? Are documents being written because the process you're following says they're needed, but it's not clear how they help you deliver what's been asked for. Are they thought of as an end in themselves? Do you sense there's a missing link?

Methodologies

There is often a focus, some might say over-reliance, on sticking to the letter of methodologies. Certainly these have their place as a framework around which to build an approach to delivering a particular project. But, and this is a big but, they aren't the be all and end all of delivering a successful project.

Command and Control

The entrenched way of managing a project is one that emphasises command and control, policing and punishment. This way of working typically involves a maze of measures (KPIs), progress reports, Gantt charts, documents. It is all too easy to lose sight of what the project is there to achieve, getting sucked down into the details of navigating the project processes, playing the system. Much energy is devoted to checking up on what has (or hasn't) been done, beating people up for missing often arbitrary dates. Is it surprising that people are motivated to meet KPI targets, leaving little space for getting on with the people they're working with, and even (dare we say it) having fun?

Why do projects fail?

So, given the environment in which projects live and breathe, what is it that leads 83 % of them to fail in delivering expectations, budget and/or on time? We were curious to pull the covers off this topic, so invited more than 20 organisations to take part in research to establish the common themes of project failure.

Four distinct sets of root causes were revealed by the research interviews. We'll talk about them a bit more, in Chapter 1. Perhaps not surprisingly, by far the biggest influence on project failure is People. In fact, if you look closely at the other three root causes, you will probably find "people causes" there somewhere too. They may not be visible on the surface, they may be deeply buried, but if you listen carefully, you will hear about them.

The impacts of failure

What are the real impacts on project success of these individual and collective failures? Some of the most common include;

- Incurring unforeseen and un-bugeted costs to achieve project objectives (£10,000s - £millions)

- Delays in achieving the expected benefits (3 months – 2 years, resource costs escalate)

- Failure to deliver the expected benefits (Return on Investment plummets)

- Negative impact on relationships with partner organisations

- Destructive impact on the organisation and its people when expectations aren't met. Personal reputations can be seriously damaged by association with a failing project

Is there a better way

It is clear that the fundamental importance of relationships, especially their nurturing whilst the seed grows at the beginning of a project, is being neglected. Minimising and managing variance are key to project delivery to satisfy the customer/end user expectations. Imagine having "no surprises".

Is there a better way to survive the stormy seas of project delivery? What happens if we look through the other end of the telescope, what do we see?

How can we manage our projects in such a way as to take care of the underlying challenges? What does it take to replace policing with cooperation, control with partnership, command with ownership and commitment?

What difference can it make if these seeds are cared for, watered and allowed to grow? What would happen if everyone involved with a project took a lead, took responsibility for their own and the team's activities?

Unlocking the treasure chest

In the course of our work with clients across private and public sectors, with small and large organisations, we have seen similar struggles arising time and time again. There are three keys to unlock the treasure chest that is the successful project;

- *Key 1:* "Begin with the end in mind"

- *Key 2:* Focus on the human factors to heal the fractures

- *Key 3:* Time invested in discovering and defining what your project is there to do, is paid back tenfold during the life of the project

For us to make a real difference, we must turn the ingrained traditional approach to project management on its head. Turn away from "managing" people and projects, leave behind policing and punishment, step back from command and control. We can choose to become a leader, whatever our role, to craft together a crystal clear picture of where a project will take us, a SatNav route to a shared destination.

There is a big difference between managing and leading projects. On the following page is a simple description of the two, that may be useful as you read this book.

Project Management	Project Leadership
■ Task Focused	■ People Focused
■ Planning	■ Providing vision
■ Setting measures and targets	■ Inspiring others
■ Reviewing Progress	■ Providing Direction
■ Understanding strengths and weaknesses	■ Aligning to common goals
■ Understanding problems and needs	■ Involving people
■ Communicating to get the task done	■ Communicating to understand individual perspectives and issues

Adapted from Warren Bennis 'On Becoming a Leader'

Why Now?

When Noah was asked to build an Ark, he was given a very clear specification for the end result, along with a definite time scale. We've researched various bible versions of the Great Flood story and there was no mention of the actual building of the Ark in any of them. However, the stories have great detail about the project scope;

[14] *Make thee an ark of gopher wood; rooms shalt thou make in the ark, and shalt pitch it within and without with pitch*

[15] *And this is the fashion which thou shalt make it of: The length of the ark shall be three hundred cubits, the breadth of it fifty cubits, and the height of it thirty cubits*

[16] *A window shalt thou make to the ark, and in a cubit shalt thou finish it above; and the door of the ark shalt thou set in the side thereof; with lower, second, and third stories shalt thou make it*

[19] *And of every living thing of all flesh, two of every sort shalt thou bring into the ark, to keep them alive with thee; they shall be male and female*

[20] *Of fowls after their kind, and of cattle after their kind, of every creeping thing of the earth after his kind, two of every sort shall come unto thee, to keep them alive*

[21] *And take thou unto thee of all food that is eaten, and thou shalt gather it to thee; and it shall be for food for thee, and for them*

And the Purpose;

[17] *And, behold, I, even I, do bring a flood of waters upon the earth, to destroy all flesh, wherein is the breath of life, from under heaven; and every thing that is in the earth shall die*

[18] *But with thee will I establish my covenant; and thou shalt come into the ark, thou, and thy sons, and thy wife, and thy sons' wives with thee*

There's no mention of how the project to build the ark was managed, reviews made and progress tracked. It was all about leadership with a clear purpose and end-point.

Perhaps this suggests that project management started out with very clear goals, specifications and time scales. Belbin identified three periods of history; pre-industrial, industrial, post-industrial. During the industrial age, management moved away from the specifics of what and instead focused tremendous energies upon the how and processes (think about how many methodologies and processes have been developed to manage projects, especially in the past 100 years). A lot of complexity has been developed, with talk about competing methodologies, processes and monitoring tools. There's a focus upon command and control of project "resources" (i.e. people), tasks, etc.

In the post-industrial age, the emphasis is moving away from huge industrialised activities, towards smaller, more agile undertakings, cottage industries. It is perhaps no accident that the vast majority of business organisations in the UK are exactly this type of small, agile, flexible unit. In this post-industrial society, there are more and more projects being started, with expectations that the thing that is delivered will have a longer operational life than before. There's this demand to constantly *"do more with less, in less time"* It is time for the way we deliver our projects to evolve to reflect this new paradigm. Perhaps we're coming full circle, back to emphasising the value of leadership, giving clear scope and purpose, providing space for those involved to deliver.

Why us?

Martin had been delivering NLP training since 1996 and Matthew had been delivering projects since 1993.

Martin was looking at ways of applying NLP tools and techniques in specific work-related contexts and had already developed Navigator – an NLP based process to help with Strategic Planning.

Matthew had been looking for ways to simplify projects. As part of this he had developed Project Fractures, which included a series of 9 key questions to ask any project. The answers to these reduce the risk of project failure.

Matthew tried out some of the NLP tools and techniques he learned on Martin's NLP Business Practitioner course with several project teams. He was stunned by how much difference it made to the people in the room each time he used them and realised that NLP could really help in all manner of situations.

Martin and Matthew began working on Project Leadership in September 2010 and realised very quickly that it would make a real difference.

By combining elements of Navigator and Project Fractures, with Leadership theories, processes and skills a simple but effective process quickly took shape.

And this is it.

How to use this book

To help you reach a good understanding of Project Leadership, we suggest that you read through this book from cover to cover.

If you're looking for some immediate insight, or you have a burning issue that just can't wait, its okay to jump straight to Chapter 18, where you can assess the situation you find yourself in and discover what can help resolve the underlying issues that you face.

Who is this book for?

Anyone who has ever had a nagging feeling that projects can be done better, that they're about more than hitting planned dates, that it would be great to actually enjoy some part of their work.

Whether you are a member of a project team, someone who is affected by what the team does, a project "manager", the sponsor of a project or the eventual customer of the results, this book will guide you towards getting more out of your involvement....

CHAPTER

01

The Big Picture...

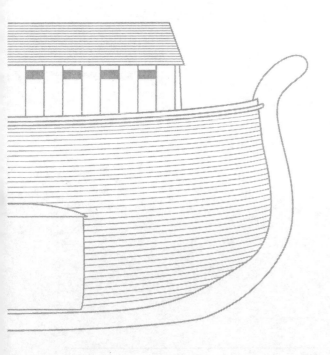

The Big Picture

We talked earlier about the situation that we often find ourselves in, when we get started with a new project, or get parachuted in to one that's already running. So many times, we're placed in a situation where the project fails, adding to the pile of projects consigned to the graveyard of under-delivery. Perhaps it's understandable that so many of them fail.

Organisations we spoke with, to satisfy our curiosity about the causes of project failure, collectively talked about four distinct sets of root causes.

Looking at the results of the conversations, we saw there was a definite overlap between the "people" set and each of the others.

Also, "people" causes were swimming underneath the surface of most, if not all, of the other sets of causes. Sometimes, you could only see the tip of the fin poking out of the water, but it was there nonetheless.

Some examples of the things that were going wrong included;

- A **change of people in key roles**, part way through. Often, they came armed with a different set of objectives, typically hidden from the rest of the team. The new people didn't have the benefit of the history and learnings that the team had gained along the way

- Roles on project teams were not well defined, or even non-existent! This was leading to an **inability to act or take decisions**

- People **did not feel empowered** or authorised to discharge their project responsibilities, irrespective of what the organisation had documented for their position

- Stakeholders were not being held to account for their actions. Many were **circumventing** agreed ways of working, taking decisions without thinking about the impact, ignoring agreements for resources and information

- Time and time again, the end customers were not getting involved during the formative stages of projects, when they could shape or influence the objectives, scope or strategy. These people were usually brought on-board at the point where they were expected to do some work. It's not surprising then that there were significant delays and changes to take account of what the eventual users really wanted

- **Widely differing expectations** about scope, deliverables and the ultimate aims existed between parties working on the same project. Seldom did anyone take the time to check that everyone had the same understanding of their goals and how to reach them

Assumptions were made during the definition of project strategy, planning and when taking decisions. No one mentioned challenging or testing these assumptions.

Blindness to the reality of getting a project done in a busy organisation was described by the words of one experienced project sponsor, *"we typically over commit to project time lines, to get a product to the market, cut corners to meet those times and then wonder why the product isn't delivered".*

Many projects didn't take the time to sort out how the team would work together, how they would measure progress, what processes they would follow.

Often, failure to deliver was directly linked to people renaging on commitments they had made during the planning, e.g. for resources, scope of work, facilities.

Many of these will sound familiar to you. Maybe you have seen similar things playing out as a project unravels. Let's look through the other end of this telescope, what do you see?

From our time spent looking through the other end of the telescope, we came to see that all projects are essentially made up of three elements;

From this vantage point, you can also see that the three keys are present, whichever of these elements you're in. You can begin with the end in mind, focus on the human factors and take time to discover what your project is there to do.

How does this fit together, what processes, tools and skills will you bring to bear? Here's the big picture of authentic project leadership, focusing on people rather than tasks;

Shortly, we will explore together the detail of each of these phases, and how this view can be used at a variety of levels of detail within your project. First, lets look at the goals of each phase. Discover and Design answer six questions that every project has to answer; why, what, how, when, who, where. Deliver puts into practice the plan to address the answers to these six questions.

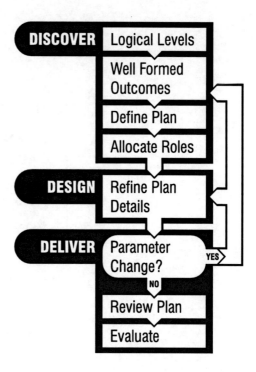

DISCOVER — Logical Levels
Well Formed Outcomes
Define Plan
Allocate Roles
DESIGN — Refine Plan Details
DELIVER — Parameter Change? YES / NO
Review Plan
Evaluate

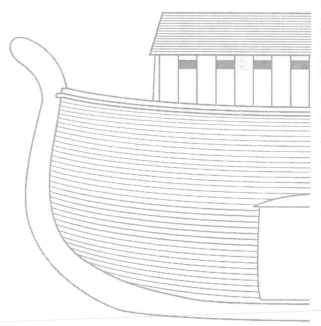

CHAPTER
02

Discover...

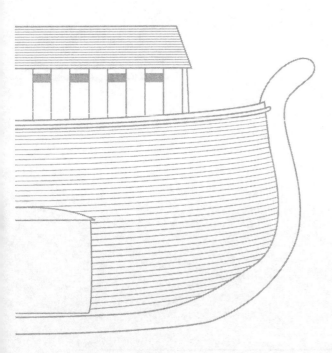

Discover

Start early, start with the end in mind

We're first going to look in some detail at the initial phase of any project; Discover.

This is all about getting everyone who should be, involved. Working together to reach a shared understanding of what your project is there to do, how it will make life better for your customer, how it will reduce the pain that people may be feeling at the moment. It's about;

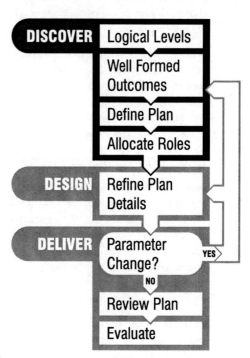

- Knowing who has some influence over your success

- Creating a clear and commonly understood end point

- Thinking about the risks you may face

- Getting everyone to the point where they can wholeheartedly commit to what you're doing together

Throughout your project, there will be a tension between those people whose preference is for reflection (transforming knowledge by structuring, ordering, sorting) and those with a preference for action (applying ideas, testing, doing). This phase, and Design, are not just about planning, they're integral parts of the project, and are packed full of actions.

You'll have noticed that the keys to your treasure chest are strongly in evidence here. This isn't a surprise, as these are the bedrock for success. Time spent learning about what your project is, and is not, about will pay huge dividends later on. Being clear about what your project is not about makes spotting and dealing with scope shift much more straightforward, more about this in Chapter 4.

If your project is breaking new ground, this phase is also likely to be about finding out what can be possible, both as an end point and as ways to get there. Some people liken this to "research and development" with a specific focus and boundary. It helps if you have at least an initial understanding of the processes that this project will change in your organisation. However, you may come to see that getting this initial understanding requires some R&D and perhaps becomes a project in its own right.

Hopefully, you have an idea (maybe not completely clear yet, that's fine) of the scope of the project. If the scope hasn't been clearly articulated, think about the need for the project, how it will benefit your organisation or end customer, what are the reasons for doing this project, at this point in time? In Chapters 6 and 7 we'll discuss the tools that you'll be using to do this. You'll probably want to ask these questions of other people, but who should you talk with?

Knowing who has influence on your success

Ben Hur is a classic Hollywood film of the 1950s, that depicts the life of a wealthy merchant prince, Ben Hur, living in Jerusalem during the early years of the current era. He is blamed for an accident that startles the horse of the Roman governor during a parade, and is condemned to the galleys. After three years as a galley slave, his self-discipline and resolve distinguish him during a sea battle, consequently he is set free and becomes a wealthy man. Later, he discovers that his mother and sister contracted leprosy while in prison and were expelled from the city. Seeking vengeance, Ben-Hur enters the upcoming chariot race before Pontius Pilate.

At the beginning of the chariot race, Ben-Hur shakes the reins and nothing happens. The four horses pulling the chariot; Aldebaran, Altaïr, Antares and Rigel, remained motionless, uncertain what was wanted of them. Ben-Hur is seen to become frustrated by the lack of coordinated action from such powerful and intelligent animals. He finally uses his whip to give them a clear message, yelling *"Giddy-up!"* The horses then roared into action.

It may already seem apparent who will be involved in the project. However, taking a little time now to consider who has influence on your success will unearth people who would have been overlooked and who have the potential to determine the success of the project.

Consider;

- Who will be taking part, informed or impacted by the project. They may be people within your organisation, suppliers, customers, clients, or perhaps end users

- Who has greater power to influence, block or support a successful outcome

- Where does the knowledge, experience and technological capability sit? These people or groups will become involved at some stage in the project, the earlier it is, the smoother the project usually runs in the long term

- Understand what information they want, and how best to communicate with them

  Some, or all, of these people will perform specific project roles, such as sponsorship, leading an activity or group of activities, recruiting others, taking part in activities.

  You may find that this happens in parallel with the next part, and that's completely fine, as they each help to clarify and refine the other.

A bit about different ways people think, learn and communicate

All the information that we receive comes to us through our five senses. We tend to favour one of these as a preferred way of creating our mind's map of reality. This usually means; seeing (visualising), hearing (auditory), or feeling (kinaesthetic). Listening to the language that people use can help a Project Leader to find out about how others think. This is a big aid to ensuring that the way you communicate with team members and stakeholders appeals to them, builds rapport (if you'd like to read more about rapport, take a look at Chapter 11). Understanding how different people prefer to receive information greatly aids the effectiveness of everything you communicate with them about. It helps keep them "on side".

Lets look at this, talk about it, see how it feels.

Visual

Some people have a preference for visual thinking, they grasp the pictures, visualise ideas readily. To persuade visual people, a drawing or helping them mentally draw a picture would be a good idea. You can use words such as; imagine, see, picture, paint, light bulb, etc. To enhance the picture, you might add more description, such as; crystal clear, sharp, colour (or black and white).

Do you see the picture?

Auditory

A while back, Matthew sent a prospective client an email, describing a proposal for a challenging piece of work that they were planning to do together. He got a very brief message in reply, simply *"sounds good to me"*. This one phrase gave a good clue to their preferred style, but probably isn't enough by itself to be certain. It does, however, allow you to focus on listening to the language they use, to find (look, hear, sniff out) other clues to their preferred style of learning.

Some of the words you'll hear that indicate an "auditory person" include; hear, strikes a chord, sounds like.

Does that ring a bell?

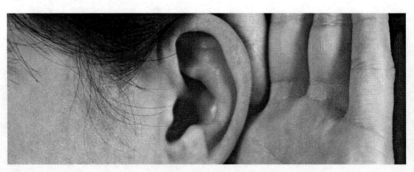

Kinaesthetic

People who prefer a kinaesthetic learning style spend the time to feel or experience an idea. The speed with which they process ideas gives a clue, as does the words they use, such as feel, hard, get a hold of, woolly, keep in touch, gut feeling.

How do you feel about that?

You may already have a sense of how this knowledge will help you communicate with the people who influence your success, develop answers to the 6 project questions and move towards a clear, shared end-point There's more about these learning styles in Chapter 10. Let's now talk about how you can go about creating the clear, shared end-point.

Creating a clear and shared end-point

Ask yourself, and other people who have an interest in the outcome;

- What the end point actually is (more specific is better)

- How you will know you have reached it

- How your business will benefit

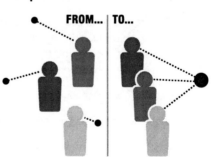

Everyone has a different picture in mind of what the end point looks like. If you ask six people to think of an elephent then ask each of them in turn to describe their elephant, you'll hear about six very different elephants. A variety of textures of sounds, feelings and images will be talked about as you come to understand each other's view of what (and where) the end is. Don't be surprised if there is some distance between the views of where you'll stop.

It's very useful, especially for your future sanity, to understand what information, actions or results will tell you that you've arrived at where you wanted to be. Many's the project that has stopped too short of the finishing tape, or continued to run after crossing the finish line. The answers you get here will, in all probability, give a clear guide when you're designing the project activities in the Design phase. You may wish to flip to Chapter 7 to discover a way to gather all this information.

Thinking about the risks you may face

Consider the risks your project may face. As you are discovering, this is often much more searching if you involve others;

- Check assumptions are valid, including assumptions that may seem "too obvious to mention"

- Think outside the immediacy of the project tasks. What is happening elsewhere in the organisation, or outside, that may present a big risk to your success

- Prioritise the criticality of risks that you've identified. Which would cause the most pain, which are most likely to occur and which can be prevented?

- Focus and plan for mitigation efforts on the most critical

Find a simple way to capture the things you learn, simple documents, flip charts. It doesn't have to be complicated, in fact "less (complicated) is more".

The picture of your end point will be coming into focus. So now is a good time to start working on defining the objectives for the project team, individuals within the project and perhaps departments that will be contributing to the successful delivery. As you're forming these objectives, take care to;

- Align the objectives you identify with the endpoint

- Check that the objectives you identify are in tune with the organisation's objectives

- describe the roles within your project, so that they're clear to those they affect, and are understood

- Include individual accountability for those working on the project, reflecting the roles that you've defined together

So, now you're in a good position to craft a first plan, outlining the big chunks of activities, the objectives that you've identified together. The rule of thumb here is to plan for the "big picture", resisting the urge to go delving into detail until the next phases.

At this point, you may as Project Leader feel a strong pull from the action focused members of your team, to "get on with doing". Do you recall talking about the tension between reflection and action earlier? It may manifest itself here as starting to create detailed plans before the end-point is clear to all. Chapter 9 shares a check list that is a great right hand man for the leader, to take care that all aspects of the project are in balance.

How long should all this take? It depends upon the size, complexity and novelty of the project, each of which will impact upon the duration. However, we've found it invariably is complete within 1 day!

Summary

Know who has the potential to influence the success of your project;

- Talk with likely influencers (within and outside your organisation) to understand what is in it for them if the project succeeds or fails

- Understand the answers to 5 of the 6 questions that all projects need to answer; why, what, when, who, where

Create a clear and shared endpoint, together with the key influencers for your project;

- What does it look like

- How will you know you've reached it

- What are the benefits of reaching it (for individuals, your business)

Consider what risks your project may face, and how you can mitigate those that are more likely to happen. Think outside the confines of the project tasks. Where else could risks arise. Where else?

Start to craft your first, high level, plan of the project. Focus on objectives, making sure they fit with those of your organisation. Focus on roles and people holding themselves accountable for their role.

As Project Leader, be aware of, and address, the pull between people on your team who prefer to take action and those who prefer reflection.

CHAPTER

03

Design...

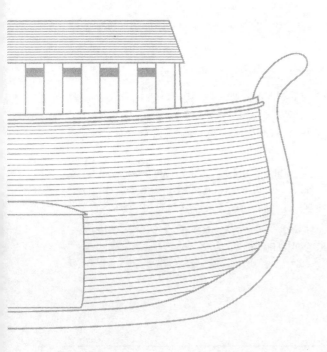

Design

Creating a strategy and a realistic, achievable plan

If you are reading this book from the start, taking action as you go, you will probably now have;

- A clearly defined and shared endpoint

- Involved the right people

- Seen where the likely (and not so likely) risks are to success

- A sketch of the plan, including objectives and roles

In this, the second phase of your project, we want to work out how we achieve the end point that's been so carefully discovered.

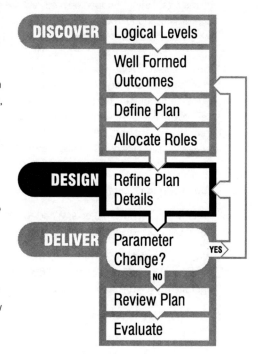

- Heeding lessons from previous experiences

- Getting concrete commitment from those who are or will be involved in delivery. In other words, planning

- Check it makes sense to continue with the project investment. Milestones (movement from stage to stage) links back to the Discover phase, looking at whether you're still heading in the right direction

You may find that one of three things happens; these steps happen one after the other; all three happen in parallel; it is an iterative process, so you re-visit each step as you find out more about the project. They're all perfectly normal routes through this phase, reflecting the wide variety of environments that we work in.

It's a good idea to involve suppliers to the project (external and internal) at this stage, to help develop and agree the plans.

Heeding lessons from previous experiences

All too often, things happen on projects and organisational memory kicks in to recall the same thing going awry on a previous project, or two, or three. We talked earlier about heeding lessons from previous experiences, here is the place to examine these lessons. As before, there is great benefit to be had from getting several people together to share experiences of similar, and dissimilar situations.

You may find it helpful to ask yourselves;

- What worked for other projects? What led to this success? What were the circumstances? Could this work for your project, or what else can you put in place for it to work?

- What actions didn't work? How did they not achieve what was expected? What could be done differently (just because it didn't work previously, doesn't always rule out an approach, given the right circumstances)

  Also, consider getting other perspectives, such as that of someone who's not involved in your project.

Planning

During this phase, you'll start to put flesh on the bones of your plan, crafted as a "big picture" during Discovery. This will help button tasks down, so there is less opportunity for scope and intent creep to occur by stealth, during the life of the project. There will certainly be pressures on your scope and intent, however with the result of the actions you take here, you're equipped to spot them, maybe before they become visible to other people, head them off at the pass or be ahead of the game in understanding them and their impact. The keys to creating successful, living, evolving plans that continue to be useful, include;

- Involving project influencers in creating and agreeing a plan

- Defining "Well Formed" project stages, activities and tasks. There's more about Well Formed Outcomes later

- Plan with coarse detail for long term stages, getting finer the nearer a stage becomes

- Consider how you will deal with changes, both big and small. How will they be described, decisions made, implemented?

- How will you, the project team, work together. Organisational norms, procedures you are expected to follow, your relative positions in the "chain of command" will all have bearing upon the way you interact

The answers you get make it possible to describe tasks in concrete terms. You can create a picture of the activity, saying what is expected to happen and why. People have something to get a hold of, to make decisions and give commitments. Afterwards, many project teams say that they 'self-police' these commitments and air problems with delivery much sooner.

The project team will, if not before, review the etiquette of working together; acceptable or expected behaviours, establish ways of working, reporting of issues, successes and progress.

Milestones

As with most things, check it makes sense to continue with the project investment.

Check which road you will take depending upon the outcome of the tasks or activities. It may be, for example, that the data generated during testing gives results that you did not expect. How will you deal with this, what direction might you take?

- Identify logical points during the plan to undertake review, take stock of progress and the path before you (e.g. before committing to the next investment). These points could occur, for example, when you progress from one stage to the next, complete a set of tests, have data about the project deliverables

- What decisions will be made during project delivery? How will decisions be made, by whom? Often, the answers to these questions will indicate the detailed activities that should be in your plan. It may mean you change your plan, where you see that new or different data are needed to take a decision. It may lead to feeling that information that you thought was essential to a decision is now not important

Putting pen to paper

At this point, you may have felt that something has been missing in all our talk about planning.

Lots of project teams or project managers dive straight in to creating a Gantt chart, using this as their project plan. Particularly the action focused people.

Certainly, Gantt charts can be a useful part of planning, to see how parts of the project relate to each other or to track progress. However, what is even more important is creating "Well Formed" stages, activities and tasks in the first place. Documenting your plan can be as simple, or as complex, as you wish. Getting everyone to share the same view of what you're doing, taking responsibility for their part, is what's important here. The documented plan, if it's useful, can be referred to often during delivery, and yes, revised somewhat too.

Valuable, living, breathing plans will usually have several common elements;

- A clear and unambiguously stated end-point
- A description of how you will get there (a strategy)
- The roles that are needed for success, and what they are responsible for taking care of
- Milestones, decision points and the data needed to take them

Recall the great work you did during Discover to really understand everyone who could influence your project's success, your stakeholders. Your planning should include communication with these people. Depending on the size of this plan, you may decide to include it as part of this document, or as a separate document (usually for more complex projects with many stakeholders).

Some of the solid results people have told Martin and Matthew they're seeing from tuning in to the questions we touched upon earlier include;

" ....we knew what was covered by 'analytical testing', and even more importantly what wasn't. As the project unfolds I can spot and challenge scope creep much more quickly"

" Getting people to agree time-lines and commit resources was so much easier"

" ... questioning how each task took us towards our goal, we saw which were at the heart of our project"

Have you looked at lessons from other projects, developed a plan with associated decision points, defined roles for everyone involved, documented it all?
If yes, now we can move on to the Delivery phase.

Bear in mind that, during the coming phase, as parameters change you can re-visit the earlier phases.

As we move on, consider the different learning styles we talked about earlier, as you work together to deliver the plan.

Summary

Learn from the successes and challenges of other projects;

- Find out what worked (and didn't work) for other projects, why, under what circumstances. Could these actions work for your project?

- Develop your plan, defining Well Formed Outcomes for each stage

- Plan with coarse detail for the parts of the plan that are further away in time, with finer detail as they approach

- Consider how you will deal with changes

- Agree how the project team will work together

Identify logical points where you will review progress with the plan, where decisions are to be taken. Understanding the decisions often indicates the activities you need to do to get there.

Document the plan with; a clear end-point, a strategy to get there, project roles, milestones and decision points with the activities needed to reach these.

CHAPTER

04

Delivery...

Delivery

Executing your plan

You will probably now have;

- Looked for lessons from other projects, to avoid repeating errors and build a more robust plan

- Created a solid plan

- Gained the commitment of everyone involved, to do their bit

- Put in place some check points during delivery

This third phase is often the most lengthy element of a project, the focus is on delivering the plan that you put together earlier.

Build it to the plan. This can sound, at least to the casual listener, as a simple thing. *"Just follow the plan..."*.

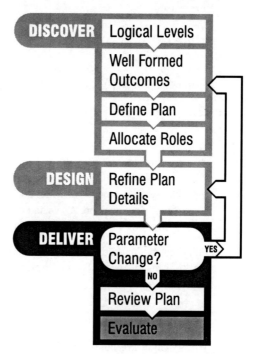

Deal with Parameter Changes. They will occur, be prepared for them and know how to manage them effectively, in a way that keeps stakeholders involved and engaged.

Review, not just at milestones. Involve the key stakeholders you identified during Discover. Adjust your plans, decision points as appropriate.

Evaluate, at the close of the project, so that the things you have learned during your project can be there for future projects to use to their advantage, just as you were able to put the lessons from other situations to good use. We talk about Evaluate in Chapter 5.

Throughout this sometimes lengthy part of your project, personal leadership is absolutely key to succeeding. We're talking here about leading within your role, no matter what you're doing related to the project, keeping motivated, taking personal responsibility for the commitments you made earlier, giving early warning of potential conflicts or issues and their resolution.

Much of the nature of Delivery is cyclical, that is; you do something, check if it is enough (makes sense, gives you some information / or not), revise based on this, execute the revised plan....

Build it

Throughout this phase, leadership from everyone involved usually shows up in two very important and valuable ways;

- Keeping motivated

- Honouring commitments

Here's where you will reap the benefits of the seeds that you took the time and thought to plant carefully during the preceding phases of your project. Keep in mind that delivery of the planned activities will likely be an iterative process, that the plan will be revised as you go along. We've heard it said that *"the agreed plan is, by definition, exactly what won't happen"*. Remember that thought and you won't go far wrong.

Carry out the activities and tasks that form your plan, remembering to pause, take stock of where you've got to, at the places you've already identified as decision points during Design.

Parameter changes

What would have happened if God decided that he would like Noah to build an aeroplane now? Fundamentally, the purpose is the same - to save two of each animal from the coming flood. Some of the work already done is still relevant. Things like the numbers of animals to house, the space they need, food requirements would probably stay the same. There would be a whole set of new challenges for Noah to overcome; discovering how to make an object fly, developing strong enough materials and a method of propulsion. You probably get the picture, have a feel for how Noah might have reacted, maybe hear the conversations he had with the project team after getting the news.

As you progress with delivering the planned project, to give your customers what they desire, it is very likely that there will be some parameter changes.

These can be things like;

- Scope changing, getting larger, new items or deliverables, perhaps reducing in size in response to external influences and drivers

- Scope creep, where small, incremental changes build up over time to drag the project away from its original target

- Changes in the skills, people, other resources available to your project. People leaving or joining the project team will have an impact upon the team dynamic

- The results of decision points taking delivery in a new direction

It's sensible to agree how you'll deal with these changes, before they happen. Usually, teams have defined their process by the end of Design. Your strategy should be based upon data or information gathered during the project

A typical approach to parameter changes may look like this;

1. Understand what the change means to your project;

   - Assess the scope and drivers for the change

   - Assess the impact on your end-point

   - Assess the impact on planned activities

   - Identify additional or changed activities

   - Negotiate the financial impact of the change

2. Decide whether to accept or reject the change, involving the appropriate people with influence on the continued success of the project.

3. These data determine which earlier phase(s) of the project you should re-visit, and who to involve.

You may discover that you should be revisiting the start, where parameters have hugely changed.

Review

Review is about validating what has been done and adjusting your course, where it makes sense to do so. And, when it feels like you've reached a milestone in your plan, use the information you gathered, to take the necessary decisions, to determine if you've achieved what you set out to do. To verify what's been built so far, as part of each milestone check consider;

- Have we achieved the outcome?

- What about risks, are there new ones, are some no longer relevant or changed in their scope, likelihood or impact? Review your earlier work to understand your risks

- Should we revise our planning or endpoint, based on what we now know?

    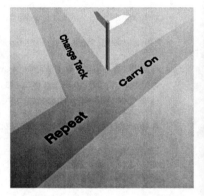

    Depending on the result of this verification, you may find it useful to return to activities, tasks and tools in Design or Discover.

Review must also look at and think about the critical skills of the project team;

- How are you working together

- What needs changing about your ways of working

- What happens within the team when challenges arise, how do behaviours support or obfuscate dealing with the situation

- Are there potential fractures to heal, in the team dynamic

    Chapters 10 to 16 discuss the key skills that will help you and your team to address these considerations.

Summary

- Follow your plan to start delivery of the project end-point

- Periodically review progress. Consider how the team is working together, how you deal with challenges , are there any issues to resolve

- Changes will very likely occur during delivery. Agree with your team how you'll deal with changes, before they start happening - define the steps you will take each change through, to understand it and decide upon actions

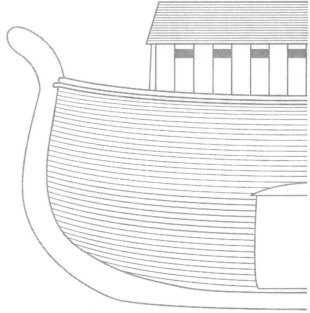

CHAPTER

05

Evaluate...

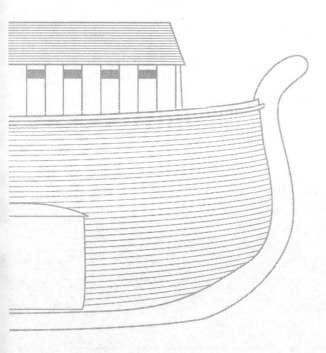

Evaluate

Your project's coming to a close, maybe you can even reach out and touch your end-point, it's that close. Before you move to your next challenge, it will probably be very useful to take a moment to take stock of all that has happened since you started to Discover.

The evaluation of what led to a project reaching its conclusion is seldom done, and even more rarely done effectively. It's all the more surprising as the way people, teams and organisations learn is by doing, reflecting on what was done and choosing to either do more of the same, or try something different, next time, depending on the reflection (the Plan - Do - Check - Act cycle).

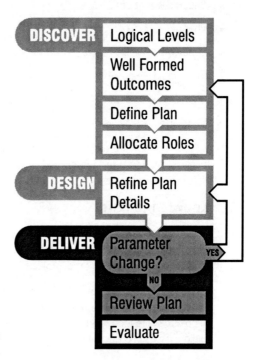

Think back to when your project was starting, to when you were finding your way, seeking to learn from the experiences and lessons of other project teams. What was that like? How did it feel? Would it have been helpful to quickly find out about the successes and challenges of other teams?

Evaluating delivered projects is an integral part of the evolution of any business. It helps paint a picture of what is happening in the organisation, across any number of projects and day to day activities. It gives a sense of where your strengths and danger zones lie. It is different from the "in-project" review, which seeks to validate what has been done, check if the tasks undertaken achieved what you wanted them to.

Evaluation is about looking back over the project to recap on what worked well, what you would do differently next time, what benefits the project has brought to you, to the team and to your organisation. It can provide a sense of closure, completion, the tying up of loose ends.

Questions to answer, as a project team include;

- What did we set out to do?

- What did we achieve?

- What worked well?

- What would we do differently next time?

- What can we take from this experience to other projects?

- What difference did we make?

As you seek out the answers, it can be helpful to think in terms of the process you followed, the tools, techniques and strategies used, how the team worked together. Here are two examples of the many ways that you may wish to use.

Knowledge Cafés

Something that you may find useful to get to the answers is a knowledge café. A great way of asking questions, especially for larger teams, it can also be used during Design, to tease out lessons from other projects.

Knowledge cafés bring people together in an open, creative environment. They can be run as meetings or workshops, with an emphasis on flowing dialogue that allows people to share ideas and learn from each other. Typically, people are encouraged to explore issues in order to build a consensus. Knowledge cafés can be as simple as;

Preparation

- Have a person facilitating the event, someone who can encourage participation

- Identify one or more questions that will be relevant to those taking part

- Decide who should be involved and invite them

- Create a comfortable environment - a café layout, perhaps with refreshments, works well

During the knowledge café

- The facilitator introduces the concept, ground rules and the question(s)

- People arrange themselves into groups, to discuss the question(s)

- Each person, in turn, shares their knowledge and experience, giving everyone an opportunity to talk

- The group continues the discussion, together

- The groups re-convene to share ideas and findings - given the reasons for holding the knowledge café, it's probably good to capture these

Afterwards

- A huge benefit of the event is what people take away with them, and the new connections they have made with other people

- Not forgetting that you have captured the learnings, answers to the questions posed, from a wide group of interested people

Case Studies

Another way to find out the answers, capture and make them available for others is to come together in writing a case study. These are often published for a broad audience, perhaps within one organisation, or for a wider community. Having a structured document makes information accessible to readers. The way a case study is written depends on the purpose and intended audience. The project team should decide on what they have to share and what their audience will be interested in hearing about.

A case study may be no more than about 1500 words, identifying the situation and explaining what was done. Here's an example of the information they may include;

- Summary

- Key learnings

- Background to the project or situation

- Main issues or problems

- What was done

- Outcomes and impacts

- Resources (material and people) used to achieve the outcomes

- Barriers, how they were overcome

- How it could be done differently / the same next time

However you chose to conduct the end of project evaluation, its a good idea to capture the results, so they are there for future teams to pick up and benefit from. Think about how the results will be stored and made available to other people. Many organisations place these documents on their Intranet or other widely accessible storage location.

We've seen how the tools fit together in our big picture. Next we will explore what each is about, what makes them so powerful for your project and how they can be used, practically, during each of the three phases. Chapter 17 shares how the tools and techniques we've just talked about about may be used.

CHAPTER

Logical Levels...

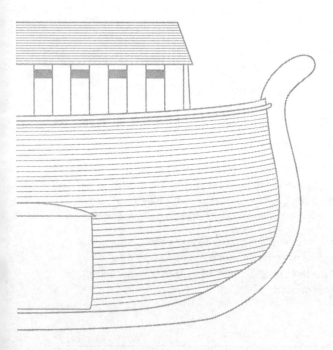

Logical Levels _____

**Logical levels of
Learning & Change.**

This concept was originally developed by Gregory Bateson and was adapted by Robert Dilts.

It refers to a hierarchy of levels of processes within an individual or group. The function of each level is to organise and direct the interactions on the level below it. Changing something on an upper level would necessarily radiate downwards precipitating change on the lower level. Changing something on a lower level could, but would not necessarily change something on an upper level.

This model is particularly useful in the Project Leadership process as an analytical tool which helps to define the big picture of the project and to create and enhance team motivation and buy-in.

Following a session where we used the process described in Chapter 17, Tracy Winser, Head of Customer Services for West Devon Borough Council and South Hams District Council said:

"We managed to agree our service objectives and design a plan to achieve them within the course of one day, a process which would normally have meant us holding several workshops. The process was creative, enjoyable and very effective and meant that the whole team could take an active part."

Logical levels helps you to take a reality check of where you are as a team at the start of the project, and define where you need to be to successfully complete the project.

Environmental level.

This involves the specific external conditions in which our behaviours and interactions take place.

These perceptions shape our experience of the where and when of a particular change and influence the way we approach a particular problem or goal. This context is geographical, physical, psychological and emotional.

Behavioural level

This is about what we do in the environment we have just described. What activities do we undertake and how do we behaviour together.

Behaviours depend on capabilities.

Capabilities level

This refers to our physical, mental and intellectual capabilities. These affect how we perceive and direct our actions (behaviour)

Within a project, what resources do we have (people, time, materials, equipment and money)?

Our capabilities are in turn shaped and coordinated by our values and belief systems.

Beliefs and Values level

What do we believe about the project and the team? What do we value – ie what is important about the project?

Identity Level

This consolidates the whole system of beliefs and values into a sense of 'self'. It has to do with our experience of who we are.

- **Environmental** factors determine the external opportunities or constraints a person, team or organisation has to react to. How does the environment affect the people in the organisation?

- **Behaviour** is made up of specific actions or reactions within the environment – what do people in the team do?

- **Capabilities** guide and give direction to behaviour – what are people able to do?

- **Beliefs** and values provide the reinforcement that supports or denies capabilities – What is true or not true about the team? What is important to the team and the people in it?

- **Identity** determines overall purpose and shapes beliefs and values through our sense of self – Who are we? What is the identity of the organisation?

- Having a clear identity as a team makes it a lot easier to define and share beliefs and values, it aids the definition of required capabilities and determines the helpful behaviours. This leads to a positive environment

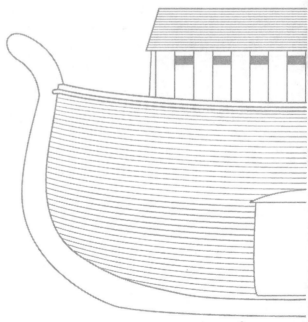

Well-Formed Outcomes...

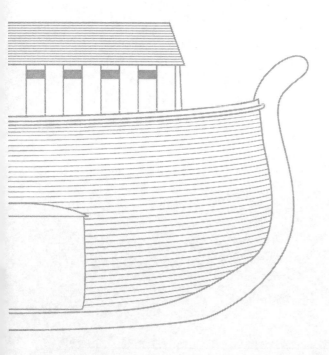

Well-Formed Outcomes _____

Having a well defined goal is crucial to the success of any project.

Most of you will have seen SMART objectives where

S – Specific

M – Measurable

A – Achievable

R – Realistic

T – Time Bound

This is a useful acronym to use when goal setting but it has a fundamental flaw.

You may have seen other letters being inserted into the acronym: Measurable becomes Measurable/Observable to take into account that behavioural changes are difficult to measure.

Achievable becomes Achievable/Agreed to try to get some buy-in from team members.

Realistic becomes Relevant because Realistic is the same as Achievable.

Martin has seen SMART become SMARTER or C-SMART and on one memorable occasion SMARTARSE objectives.

Some years ago Martin was working for a chemical company in the North West, and he arrived early to prepare for the course as he always does and consequently there was no receptionist. There was a security guard on the desk and he said that they'd have to wait for the receptionist to arrive before Martin could get into the room.

So they just started chatting and the guard asked where Martin had driven up from. He said he'd come up from Cornwall and the Guard said, *"Cornwall, oh right we nearly bought a Guesthouse in St Ives."*

Being curious Martin asked, *"Nearly? What happened?"*

The Guard replied *"Well, we've always had this dream to buy a Guesthouse and we love St Ives, we've been going on holiday there for ever and it's a lovely place and we love the light and sea and everything about it. It's fantastic and we had this dream that were going to retire there, buy a Guesthouse and live out our days running a Guesthouse in St Ives."*

It turned out that before he'd retired and become a security guard he was a manager in an engineering company and he said that they knew about SMART goals because he'd been on all the courses, "*So me and the wife sat down and we said right let's change this from being a dream into a goal. Let's actually make it happen.*"

So the Guard asked the question "What do we actually want? Well we want a Guesthouse with enough accommodation to be able to give us enough income to be able to get a mortgage and live and do what we need to do. It's got to have a sea view. It's got to have enough car parking spaces for the guests' which if you know St Ives is very very difficult. It's got to be running well at the minute. It's got to be in good order because we don't want to spend a lot of money on maintaining it."

So they had defined a lot of very specific needs there.

"Was it measurable?" he went on, *"Yes, of course it's measurable because we'll be able to look at the books. We'll know whether there's enough of an income. Is it observable? Yes we'll be able to see it, we can see whether there's a sea view, we can count the number of parking spaces and so on. Is it achievable? Well we think so because we've looked at the kind of prices of guest houses down there."*

This was going back a few years. *"And we know what our house is worth and what my pension's going to be worth, so financially yes we think it's achievable. Do we both want to do it? Absolutely. We've wanted this since we were first married. It is our life goal and now we think it's actually achievable. Is it realistic? Is it relevant? Well, yes because it's our life goal. It's what we really really want. This is what's going to make us the happiest that we can be. When do we want it? The day that I retire we want to move directly into this guest house."*

He paused, looked meaningfully at Martin and carried on.

"We wrote it all down because we knew that writing goals down makes them more likely to achieve them. So off we went down to St Ives. We looked in all the estate agents, got all the magazines, all the books and all the rest of it. Information from the estate agents and very quickly found the exact place, it was almost like it was meant to be. We found the place with the sea view, the car park, with enough beds to produce the income. It was pretty full for the next year so we didn't even have to do any marketing. The books showed that it had a good income. Everything was perfect. We put our house on the market and it sold within two days. We put an offer in on the guest house. That was accepted. We started to go through the whole process of buying this place, survey done and all the rest of it and just when we were about to sign the contracts my wife said 'I don't want to move 400 miles away from the grandchildren."

So they didn't go. So what went wrong? It was definitely agreed when they went through the process, there's no doubt about that.

The Goal was Specific, It was Measurable and Observable, it was agreed, achievable and relevant and it was Time Constrained.

Deep down however, his wife didn't want the goal.

The problem with SMART goals is that the process doesn't take the unconscious into account.

This is why we often 'sabotage' our goals. They sound like a good idea, they make sense and yet we find it impossible to achieve them. A classic example of this are New Year's Resolutions – it makes sense to give up smoking or lose weight but at an unconscious level we still enjoy smoking or eating unhealthy food and so we soon revert back to our old behaviour because nothing has changed at an unconscious level.

To get buy-in from a team, this problem is magnified and as a Project Leader you will often find most of your time is spent chasing people to get the job done.

If you can get everyone to buy-in to the outcome of the project, the task is completed much more easily.

The Well-Formed Outcome process takes the valuable parts of SMART and adds questions to get buy-in at an unconscious level.

Goal setting itself is important and this process will help to align the conscious and the unconscious and help you to set a goal for yourself and your team which you're much more likely to achieve.

Be Specific

First of all, make sure you're very specific about the goal that you want to achieve in terms of your outcome. Make sure you state it in the positive. Because the unconscious doesn't process negatives directly. So if I say to you *"don't think of a cat"*, what comes to mind? So if you say to yourself, *"I don't want to be working here in this job in 3 years time"*, there's a very good chance that you'll still be here in 3 years time doing this job. So make sure that the goal you set for yourself is stated as a positive.

When Martin and his Family re-located to Cornwall they wanted 'a four bedroom detached house with a garden and a garage in St Agnes in Cornwall'

Where Are You Now?

The next step is to be aware of where you are now in relation to this goal.

Martin and his family were in Northwich in Cheshire. 330 miles from St Agnes. they had transferable skills, they had equity in the house so they had the ability to make it happen.

How Will You Know When You Have Achieved It?

The next step is to imagine you've achieved the goal. This is the measurable bit. The evidence. How will you know when you've achieved your goal. What will you see when you've achieved it? What will you hear when you've achieved it? How will you feel when you've achieved it?

The purpose of defining the evidence in that way is that you are using all your key senses to make the outcome more real and compelling, which becomes motivational.

For example, Martin could say that *"We want to move to Cornwall"*

Or he could picture himself on the slipway going down to the beach and see himself there looking out to sea, the sun's shining and the sea is blue, that unique Cornish blue, and the surf is bright white with the sun glinting off it and off the spray and on the cliffs to the right there's a purple and yellow cloud with the heather and gorse all mixed together and he can see the children running around and playing. He can hear the surf booming as it hits the rocks and crashing onto the beach and that kind of sucking noise as it runs back out again. He can hear the children squealing as they run in and out of the water because it's cold and the seagulls circling around, crying. He can feel the warmth of the sun and there's a slight breeze and he can feel the sand beneath his feet, which is warm and he's just feeling relaxed, happy and comfortable.

 Which is the most compelling?

When you create the evidence for yourself, make it something you really want to achieve. Make it vivid. Make it compelling. Make it something really aspirational, rather than something grey and dull.

And then when you've done that, made it really compelling, ask yourself will there be any other evidence? How else will I know? Maybe the bank balance?

For What Purpose?

 Ask yourself what achieving this goal will get for you? Or what it will allow you to do? Because a goal isn't an end in itself. People don't do the lottery just for the money. They don't win millions of pounds and then just pile it all up on the floor to look at.

What were Martin and his family moving to Cornwall for? Well, they wanted a better standard of life, they wanted a more outdoors life, they wanted to be able to go to the sea and go surfing, to take the children down to the beach. They wanted a more free life for the kids so they could go out more on their own. They wanted to be part of a close knit community and to contribute to that community.

Is the Goal Within Your Control?

Is the goal self-maintained? Are you in control of it? Is the team able to achieve the goal or is the organisation able to achieve the goal? Does it rely on us getting £X million from the Board to achieve it?

Was moving to Cornwall within their control? Absolutely!

What is the context?

When do you want to achieve this goal? Where do you want it? With whom? Setting the context is crucial to ensure you achieve the right goal at the right time.

Who did Martin and his Partner want in Cornwall with them? The children. Where did they want it? They wanted to be in St Agnes in Cornwall. And when did they want it? 31st December 1999. They wanted to be in their house in St Agnes by then.

Having an end point really helps to focus on both a conscious and unconscious level.

What Resources Are Needed?

What resources do you need to achieve the goal? What have you got at the moment? What extra resources do you need? And have you ever done it before? Do you know anyone that's done it who could help with advice?

They'd moved house before but hadn't moved to Cornwall so they could learn from that experience. They also knew people who had relocated to Cornwall so could ask them.

They ran a business that, although most clients were in the North West could easily be UK wide or Cornwall specific.

Ecology Check

What will you gain when you achieve this goal? What will you lose? This was the question that the security guard didn't ask. There is no gain without loss and no loss without gain.

What effect will this change have on the people around you? Is that change acceptable?

Moving to Cornwall was going to mean a big change for Martin and his Partner's children, and they had to explore whether that was acceptable. If the children really didn't want to move they decided that they would not move until the children had left home.

Martin and his family moved into their house in St Agnes in March 1999. It wasn't a four bedroom detached house with a garden and garage but it met their needs and the transition to Cornwall went really well (they're still there).

Lets recap on the process that got Martin and his family to Cornwall

1. **State the goal as a positive.**

   What specifically do you want?

   The unconscious doesn't process negatives directly (Don't think of a cat).

   If you set your goal as a negative (I don't want to be working here in 3 years time) there is a very good chance that you will not achieve it and will find yourself still there in 3 years time.

2. **Specify present situation.**

   Where are you now? against the achievement of the goal

3. **Specify outcome.**

   What will you see, hear, feel, when you have achieved it?

   Make it compelling and motivating

4. **Other evidence**

   How will you know when you have it? Will there be any documentary evidence additional to the see, hear and feel.

5. **For what purpose?**

   What will this outcome get for you or allow you to do?

   No goal is an end in itself – no-one plays the lottery just to win the money, they play it to have what the money can get for them.

6. Is it self-initiated?

Are you in control?

If not, what needs to happen for you to be in control?

7. What is the desired context?

Where, when, how, and with whom do you want it?

What date, and time will you have achieved the goal.

8. What resources are needed?

What do you have now, and what do you need to get your outcome?

What money, time, people, skills, equipment do you have?

9. Is it ecologically sound?

For what purpose do you want this?

What will you gain or lose if you have it?

Involving your team in setting the Well Formed Outcome for the project will have a motivating effect for the team and will develop a real clarity and shared purpose.

Getting the team's buy-in at this stage in the project will make a huge difference throughout the project and will not only aid the achievement of the goal but will help you as the Project Leader to get the most out of your team throughout the process.

CHAPTER

Time line...

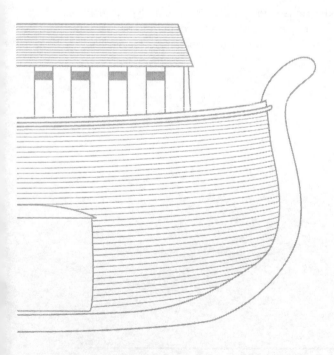

Time line _____

For many centuries, we have been trying to make sense of our relationship with time. Aristotle, who died in 384 BC wrote that: *"Western minds represent time as a straight line upon which we stand with our gaze directed forward; before us we have the future and behind us the past. On this line we can unequivocally define all tenses by means of points. The present is the point on which we are standing, the future is found on some point in front of us"*

In his book Foundations of Psychology, William James likened our experiences to a string of beads, with the beads being experiences, and the string representing time passing.

In the 1980s, a lot of research was carried out into people's perception of time and how that perception affected their lives. During this research it was discovered that people with different functions within a team or organisation often had different ways of relating to and indeed, perceiving time.

People with more concrete roles such as production, or project management tended to see time in a linear way with a clear progression.

It is useful to utilise this, to work **with** the way that we think, rather than try to work against it.

Imagine a line painted on the floor to represent time passing. This could represent the duration of the project.

The 'beads' could be activities which need to be completed as part of the project. There will be a logical progression of these activities – some things will need to be completed before other activities can occur.

It would be possible to use this approach to review a project – to analyse what happened in which order.

It is also possible to use this approach to plan an activity or project.

'In time' and 'Through Time'

Although people may view time in a linear way, the way these timelines are perceived will differ.

These people can be grouped as 'In Time' people and 'Through Time' people.

Through Time

Through Time people can see their timeline moving from left to right (or right to left) in front of them.

Through Time people tend to like lists, they will be on time always (and get angry if you are not), will love to use their organisers and will want to complete things...now!

They can sometimes be overwhelmed by all the things that need to be done and can lose focus on the immediate task in hand.

In Time

In Time people see their timeline running from behind to in front (or front to behind) with themselves on the timeline.

In Time people are open ended, they don't want lists or to be tied down in any way. They tend to be less effective planners and aren't naturally good at goal setting.

They are very good at focusing on the 'now' and are less distracted by what needs to be done next.

They may have several things on the go at the same time and don't always need completion.

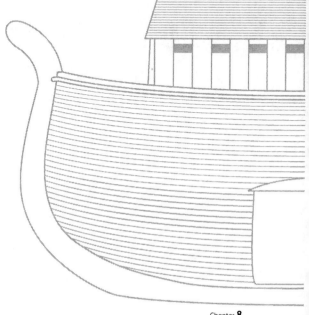

How to build an **ARK**

CHAPTER

Leadership...

Leadership

There is a big difference between Project Management and Project Leadership and reflects the fact that most projects are carried out by a team, rather than by an individual.

Project Management	Project Leadership
■ Task Focused	■ People Focused
■ Planning	■ Providing vision
■ Setting measures and targets	■ Inspiring others
■ Reviewing Progress	■ Providing Direction
■ Understanding strengths and weaknesses	■ Aligning to common goals
■ Understanding problems and needs	■ Involving people
■ Communicating to get the task done	■ Communicating to understand individual perspectives and issues

Adapted from Warren Bennis 'On Becoming a Leader'

There are a number of different definitions of leadership some of which are outlined below.

" Leadership denotes unleashing energy, building, freeing and growing"

Tom Peters

" Leadership is the art of getting more from people than they think they are capable of giving"

Sir Raymond Lygo

" Management is about doing things right, leadership is about doing the right things"

Warren Bennis

" A leader is a dealer in hope"　　　　　Napoleon Bonaparte

*" Leadership is a combination of strategy and character.
If you must be without one, be without the strategy"*

Gen. H. Norman Schwarzkopf

" Leadership is influence - nothing more, nothing less"

John Maxwell

The fact that there are so many definitions of leadership is a good illustration of the fact that it is very difficult to define; but there certainly seems to be a view that it is very different to management.

In this section we look at two concepts of leadership and explore how we can utilise these to improve the success of projects.

Action Centred Leadership

Professor John Adair used his research in both the armed forces and industry to identify what successful leaders actually do. He then developed this functional model using the three circles diagram.

A leader is a person who is appointed to achieve results with and through other people. Those results may be project based, or operationally based, or even strategic in nature.

Whether or not these results are achieved and how much a leader needs to influence others in order to gain results depends on varying factors.

These include:

- The nature of the task in question

- The skills and needs (both technical and personal) of the individuals concerned

- The way in which those individuals integrate as a team

Efficient leadership, therefore, requires flexibility and an awareness of these different requirements in order to strike a balance for the particular job in hand. This balancing act is illustrated by Adair's three overlapping circles.

Individual:
Satisfying the requirements of individuals within the team.

Team:
Nurturing and motivating the team as a whole.

Task:
Ensuring that the task is achieved.

Obviously these needs sometimes conflict with each other and one area will often require more attention than others.

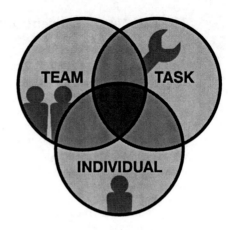

Sometimes, there is a need to focus on one circle; a new starter means that you need to look after them and spend time on their induction. A problem with the team means that you need to concentrate on developing the team and production pressures can mean that you need to focus all your efforts on completing the task.

It is crucial to achieve a long-term balance between all three and to ensure that any imbalances are resolved as quickly as possible. In this way, if one person demands a heavy input of time and energy for a while, the others will adapt - knowing that their requirements are also being looked after and will be met within the foreseeable future.

The key is that when this happens, you put effort into the other circles to redress the balance.

When you've been overly focused on the task, for example, you then need to look after the team and the individuals once the task is complete.

For example, a client of Martin's had an extremely tight deadline to meet and when he went to visit them, there was only one person in the office building. Everyone else, the Chairman, sales staff, HR, R&D, every member of the organisation was in the production area packing the products to meet the order – the Task took priority.

At the end of the week, the deadline having been met, a fleet of buses and taxis arrived to take all of the staff to a hotel for a party arranged and paid for by the Board as a thanks for all the effort. – the Team took priority

The following week, the MD went round the factory with a box full of baseball caps with 'Thanks' emblazoned on each one. He individually thanked every employee shook their hands and gave them a cap which many of them were still wearing 12 months later. – the Individual took priority

The Dangers of concentrating on:

The Task: The Leader loses focus on the team and the individuals; the team becomes dysfunctional and de-motivated. It becomes less effective and so the leader ends up doing more and more of the task him/herself. Individuals become more and more de-motivated and may eventually leave. Individuals need to have far more contact with the leader and need to be continually chased for results to be achieved.

The Team: The Leader loses focus on the task which becomes less well done, or not done at all. Individuals begin to get fed up because there is no sense of achievement. Individual performance may suffer as they require more and more input from the leader.

Some Individuals: The Leader loses focus on the other team members, the team as a whole and the task. The team becomes disillusioned and there is more individual conflict. The task becomes more and more difficult to complete effectively.

Transactional v Transformational Leadership

Transactional Leadership

Transactional Leadership is based on a set of assumptions:

- People are motivated by reward and punishment

- Social systems work best with a clear chain of command

- When people agree to do a task they cede all authority to their manager

- The main purpose for any employee is to do what they are told

- The transactional leader creates a clear structure. Employees are in no doubt as to what is expected of them and of the potential rewards/punishments (through formal disciplinary systems)

- The transaction begins when the employee joins the project team and the leader is given authority over the individuals

- When work is allocated the employee is considered to be responsible for outcomes – even when they have no control over the resources. When things go wrong blame is allocated to the employee

- The transactional leader often assumes that if something is working well then it needs little attention thus employees only have contact with the manager when things are going wrong

- Typical Project Management follows a Transactional model

Transformational Leadership

Transformational Leadership is also based on a set of assumptions:

- People will follow a person who inspires them

- A person with vision and passion can achieve great things

- The best way to get things done is by injecting enthusiasm and energy

Working for a transformational Leader can be very enjoyable as they put passion and energy into everything they do. They want to support people to succeed.

Transformational Leadership starts with a vision for the future, the next step is to sell that vision and create "followers" – this phase takes energy and commitment from the leader.

The next stage is to find a way forward. The transformational leader will either have a plan and work to encourage people to follow it or will negotiate a plan with the team. The best results are obtained when the team are involved in developing the plan.

Finally, transformational Leaders will lead visibly until the project is achieved. They will work hard to provide direction, support and motivation. They will balance their efforts between the achievement of the task and the well being of the team and its members.

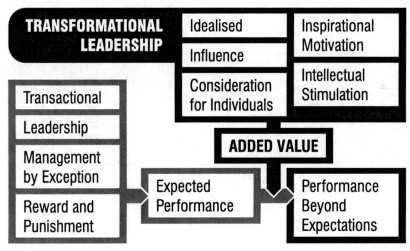

Adapted from Bass and Avolio

The Project Leadership **Checklist**

Key Actions	Task	Team	Individual
Discover	☐ Logical Level	☐ Hold team meetings and share commitment	☐ Clarify objectives ☐ Gain acceptance
	☐ Well formed ☐ Outcomes	☐ Consult ☐ Develop suggestions	☐ Encourage ideas ☐ Assess Skills
Design	☐ Define Plan ☐ Priorities ☐ Time Scales ☐ Standards	☐ Structure	☐ Allocate Jobs ☐ Delegate ☐ Set Targets
	☐ Refine Plan ☐ Objectives ☐ Describe Plan	☐ Explain decisions ☐ Answer questions ☐ Check understanding	☐ Listen ☐ Enthuse
Deliver	☐ Assess progress ☐ Review parameters ☐ Maintain standards	☐ Coordinate ☐ Reconcile conflict	☐ Advise ☐ Assist ☐ Reassure ☐ Counsel ☐ Dicipline ☐ Recognise Effort
	☐ Summarise ☐ Review ☐ Objectives ☐ Re-plan if necessary	☐ Recognise and gain from success ☐ Learn from mistakes	☐ Appraise preformance ☐ Give praise ☐ Guide and train

This checklist can help you to prioritise your efforts to ensure you consistently meet the needs of the Task, the Team and each individual in the team.

64

Key Skills

In Chapters 10 to 16 we introduce the key skills which will help you to be more effective as a Project Leader. We will not go into detail of the skills – this is another book in itself! We hope that you will be able to analyse your own level of skills against all of these key skills which will help you define any development needs you may have.

The Key Skills we will be covering are:

- Communication

- Rapport Building

- Questioning

- Giving and Receiving Feedback

- Active Listening

- Motivation and Delegation, and

- Team building

CHAPTER

10

Communication...

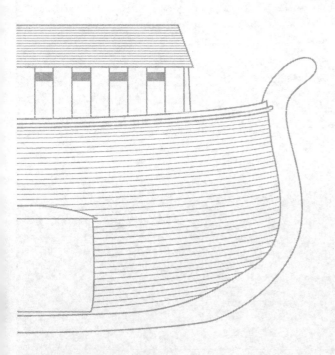

Communication _____

Effective communication is absolutely crucial to the successful leading of a project – which is why it is first on our list.

It can be defined as:

*"The transfer of information from one person to another to create **mutual understanding**"*

The final phrase is the key. Both parties have to have an exactly matching understanding of the information. This sounds obvious, but it very often doesn't happen.

Ask ten people to picture an 'Elephant' you will get ten different pictures. These will range from still to moving pictures, African or Indian elephants, cartoons, ornaments, line drawings and many others.

If that is true for a single word, image how we interpret a whole sentence!

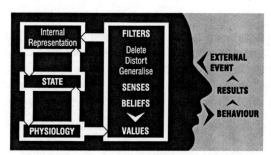

We choose our communication based on the way we respond to external events. We take information in through the senses and this information is filtered – we choose which pieces of this information to delete, distort or generalise.

We **delete** information that doesn't fit our 'map of the world' for instance, if you have a strong belief that there is no such thing as a pure white horse, you may not even notice the one in the field across the road.

We **distort** the reality around us based on our map of the world. An example of this is something Martin calls 'new car syndrome' – have you ever bought a car and suddenly seen lots of the same make and model on the road? The owners haven't all suddenly gone out and bought the same car as you, you have distorted the information you have been receiving from the outside world.

We also **generalise** about the world around us. When someone asks you to picture an elephant, you generalise that when someone asks you that question the picture they mean is the one you have in your head – because that's what the word elephant means, isn't it?

Once we have filtered all this information we form our **internal representation** of the information. This is, to us, what the message **means** – which is almost certainly different to the message the person communicating it wants us to receive. There will probably be an overlap though. For instance, when people are picturing an elephant, although they will be very different images, they will probably all be elephant shaped.

This internal representation determines how we feel about the situation which also affects our physiology. If we receive a message from our team leader which we feel has unrealistic aims, we will feel anxious and that affects us physiologically, causing the fight or flight response. This will affect the way we communicate our response – and the response we get.

When we interact with the outside world, we can only use the senses – we can only see, hear, touch, taste or smell the world around us.

When we **think** about the outside world, we can only represent it in terms of those senses. We can only remember what we saw, heard, smelled, tasted or touched. We can also only imagine what the future will be like by what we will see, hear, touch, taste or smell.

These are called **Representational Systems** and, although we use all of them, we also have preferences. Some of us prefer to think in pictures (**Visual Representational System**), some of us prefer to think in sounds (**Auditory**), some of us prefer to think in feelings (**Kinaesthetic**) some of us prefer to think logically (**Auditory** Digital) and some of us (very rare) prefer to think in smell and taste (**Olfactory/Gustatory**).

We don't just prefer to think in these Rep. Systems, we prefer to **take information** in with them.

We also tend to **communicate** using our preference.

This can cause problems of course. If we have a preference for an **auditory** Rep. System, we will be switching off any **visual or kinaesthetic** people.

For example, Martin used to have a girlfriend who, when he brought flowers home would take them from him saying "oh, flowers, thanks" in an almost dismissive way.

After they split up Martin realised that he was very visual, so a bunch of bright yellow daffodils was the perfect way of demonstrating his love. She was very kinaesthetic so a hug would have been the perfect way for her to appreciate his love. (And would have saved him lots of money!).

When they split up they said it was because they didn't communicate – which was completely true. They got together because they shared interests, sense of humour, beliefs and values but the way they communicated them to each other was like using different languages.

Visual

People who are visual often stand or sit with their heads and/or bodies erect, with their eyes up. They will be breathing from the top of their lungs. They often sit forward in their chair and tend to be organised, neat, well-groomed and orderly. They memorise by seeing pictures, and are less distracted by noise. They often have trouble remembering verbal instruction because their minds tend to wander A visual person will be interested in how your program looks. Appearances are important to them. They are often thin and wiry.

Auditory

People who are auditory will move their eyes sideways. They breathe from the middle of their chest. They typically talk to themselves, and are easily distracted by noise (some even move their lips when they talk to themselves.) They can repeat things back to you easily, they learn by listening, and usually like music and talking on the phone. They memorise by steps, procedures, and sequences(sequentially.) The auditory person likes to be told how they are doing, and responds to a certain tone of voice or set of words. They will be interested in what you have to say about your program.

Kinaesthetic

People who are kinaesthetic will typically be breathing from the bottom of their lungs, so you will see their stomach go in and out when they breathe. They often move and talk slowly. They respond to physical rewards, and touching. They also stand closer to people than a visual person. They memorise by doing or walking through something. They will be interested in your program if it "feels right".

Auditory Digital

This person will spend a fair amount of time talking to themselves. They will want to know if your program "makes sense". The auditory digital person can exhibit characteristics of other major representational systems.

Predicates

These are the words people use to describe their experiences and thought processes. They can give a valuable clue to the Representation System being used at that time.

Visual	Auditory	Kinaesthetic	Unspecified
See	hear	feel	sense
look	listen	touch	experience
view	sound(s)	grasp	understand
appear	make music	get hold of	think
show	harmonise	slip through	learn
dawn	tune in/out	catch on	process
reveal	be all ears	tap into	decide
envision	rings a bell	make contact	motivate
illuminate	silence	throw out	consider
imagine	be heard	turn around	change
clear	resonate	hard	perceive
foggy	deaf	unfeeling	insensitive
focused	mellifluous	concrete	distinct
hazy	dissonance	scrape	conceive
crystal	question	get at handle	know
picture	unhearing	solid	sense

Predicate Phrases

As with the Predicates, the following phrases can give a good indication of the thought processes being used.

It is important not to rely solely on these however but to use them as part of the information you are receiving to help you determine their preferred Representation System.

Visual	Auditory	Kinaesthetic
An eyeful	Afterthought	All washed up
Appears to me	Blabbermouth	Boils down to
Beyond a shadow of a doubt	Clear as a bell	Chip off the old block
Bird's eye view	Clearly expressed	Come to grips with
Catch a glimpse of	Call on	Control yourself
Clear cut	describe in detail	Cool/calm/collected
Dim view	Earful	Firm foundations
Flashed on	Give an account of	Get a handle on
Get a perspective on	Give me your ear	Get a load of this
Get a scope on	Grant an audience	Get in touch with
Hazy idea	Heard voices	Get the drift of
Horse of a different colour	Hidden message	Get your goat
In light of	Hold your tongue	Hand in hand
In person	Idle talk	Hang in there
In view of	Inquire into	Heated argument
Looks like	Keynote speaker	Hold it!
Make a scene	Loud and clear	Hold on!
Mental image	Manner of speaking	Hothead
Mental picture	Pay attention to	Keep your shirt on
Mind's eye	Power of speech	Know-how

Visual	Auditory	Kinaesthetic
Naked eye	Purrs like a kitten	Lay cards on table
Paint a picture	State your purpose	Pain-in the neck
See to it	Tattle-tale	Pull some strings
Shortsighted	To tell the truth	Sharp as a tack
Showing off	Tongue-tied	Slipped my mind
Sight for sore eyes	Tuned in/tuned out	Smooth operator
Staring off into space	Unheard of	So-so
Take a peek	Utterly	Start from scratch
Tunnel vision	Voiced an opinion	Stiff upper lip
Under your nose	Well informed	Too much of a hassle
Up front	Within hearing	Topsy-turvy

It is important to consider preferred Representation Systems when communicating with project team members and stakeholders.

We don't just communicate our message in words – we use Body Language and tone of voice as well to get our message across.

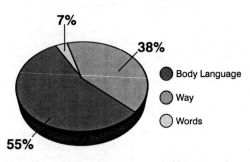

In fact, the words are the least important part of our communication in terms of the effect our message has on other people.

Albert Mehrabian's research into the communication of feelings and attitudes developed this model.

Words

The words we use are important – they help us to give information and to convey understanding. The words we use are the basic building blocks of our communication and we should consciously choose the types of words we use depending on who we are talking to and the circumstances in which we are talking to them. For example: We use technical terms and jargon when discussing matters with someone who shares our understanding but we use simpler language when we are explaining something complex to a person who is unfamiliar with the concepts.

Way

The words we use are important but the way in which we say them is more important still. The tone of voice we use conveys our emotion – if we are hurt, stressed, angry or happy it will come over in our tone of voice. As leaders we need to be very careful to use the tone of voice we intended to rather than "leak" emotions that are not particularly appropriate.

But the way we say things is about more than just tone of voice – it includes the speed and the volume at which we speak and any accent we may have, all of which can have an impact on the message we are trying to deliver.

Body Language

Our body language conveys a great deal about us – it tells people what mood we are in, whether or not we are in a hurry, if we are likely to be receptive to their ideas etc. The problem is that much of the interpretation of body language takes place at an unconscious level – we are not aware that we have made a decision or a judgement about someone or what they mean, even though we have at an unconscious level which affects our **internal representation**. Have you ever walked into a room at a party, or for a meeting and thought *"I'll go and talk to them, they seem ok"* or *"I'm not going anywhere near them"*. How have you made that decision? You base it on how they look, and your experience of what that facial expression, body posture meant when someone else exhibited it.

Be very aware of the affect your body language has on people when you talk to them – and check it out.

If someone looks bored, or unhappy with what you have just said, check it out. They will either say that they're not bored, or that they are bored. Either way, you now have some clear information to work with.

In summary, effective communication is crucial for you to successfully lead any project. It is worth thinking about and planning how you are going to communicate to your team and stakeholders.

Remember that, if people cannot see your body language they will invent it (have you ever seen a picture of a DJ and thought *"I didn't think he looked like that?"* or met someone face to face when you have only spoken to them on the phone and been surprised at their appearance? You have invented 38% of the meaning of the message!

Even more worrying is that people will invent 93% of the message if they don't have the body language or the tone of voice. Do you use email?

Most of the time, when we are communicating, we try to drag people into our world so that they see the world the way that we do. If we want to be **really** effective as a communicator, we need to step out of our world and into the other person's world. See the world through their eyes and only then can we communicate effectively and achieve mutual understanding.

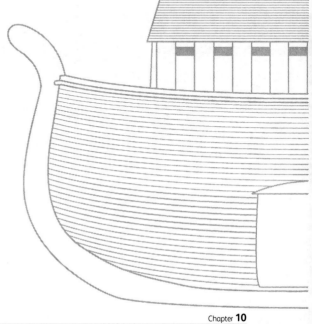

CHAPTER

11

Rapport Building...

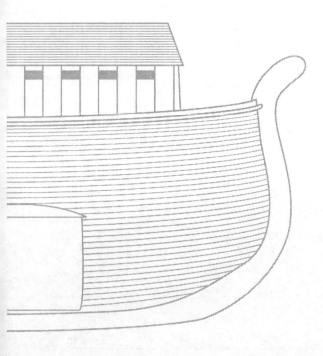

Rapport Building _____

The Concise Oxford English Dictionary defines rapport as:

"A Close and harmonious relationship in which there is a common understanding"

There are probably some people you find it really easy to communicate with and motivate. There are probably some other people you find really difficult to motivate and communicate with.

If you think about your friends, what is it about them that makes them friends?

Do you work in the same place?

Do you share interests?

Do you have the same sense of humour and laugh at the same things?

Do you have similar backgrounds?

Do you share beliefs and values?

You probably answered yes to most, if not all of these questions.

With some friends you probably answered yes to more questions than for others. We will look at why that is later.

The fact is that we are attracted to people like us. We **like** people who are like us.

We are much more likely to work well with people we have a natural rapport with. So the people we have to lead who we **like** and who like us are much more likely to respond to our ideas, direction and proposals.

Unfortunately, we are not like everyone in the world, and often have to lead teams with people who are not like us – and sometimes, even with people we don't actually like.

Taking time to find out about your team members, and demonstrating how you are like them by finding common areas of interest and experience is very helpful when building rapport.

A more subtle technique is matching your behaviour to theirs – copying their body language and tone of voice.

This may feel really clumsy at first but is actually the most effective way of creating rapport.

The most effective process for influencing others and building rapport is:

Pace – build rapport initially by matching Body Language, Tone of Voice and Words

Pace – demonstrate that you understand what it is like to be them.

Lead - only when you have moved through the first two stages can you lead another person, or group of people in the direction you want them to go.

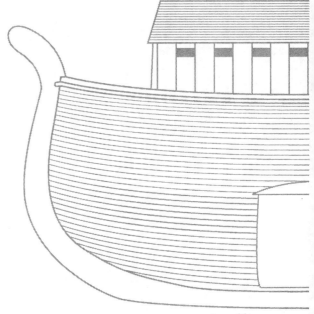

How to build an **ARK**

CHAPTER

12

Questioning...

Questioning _____

Asking questions elicits information. Asking the right questions elicits the right information.

There are many different type of question, each type of question will elicit a different type, or amount of information.

Question Types

Closed Questions

It can be very frustrating when the person we are talking to gives one- word answers to every question asked. However the fault may lie more with the questioner than with the respondent. Closed questions can usually only be answered with a simple yes or no.

E.g. *"Did you come by car?"* If the respondent answers *"yes"* then you have your information but if the respondent answers *"no"* then you have to ask a further question (or 5) in order to find out how they travelled.

An open question will get you more information but the closed question does have a role. Sometimes a simple *"yes"* or *"no"* is all that is required, especially if you are simply checking your understanding of the situation or summarising what has been said so far.

E.g. *"Are you warm enough?"*

"Yes"

Open Questions

Open questions are used to draw out more information on a subject and are designed to encourage the speaker to elaborate. Open questions typically start with the words who, why, where, what, when or how.

" *I had six honest serving men. They taught me all I know. Their names are what and why and when and how and where and who* "

Rudyard Kipling

E.g. *"How did you get here today?"*

This leaves the respondent free to tell you how they got here.

This also demonstrates the importance of asking the right question to get the information you need. There are several answers to the question *"How did you get here today?"*

"I came by car"

" I used the A30 and then the A38"

" I left school at 16 with no qualifications and went straight into my first job where I worked for 5 years, after that I..."

Sometimes open questions can seem a little interrogatory avoid using questions starting with *"why?"*

Why? Is a justifier and is almost guaranteed to elicit a defensive response.

E.g. *"Why did you do that?"* may get you the information that you need but get the tone wrong and it implies that you are allocating blame and you may just get a *"I don't know"* response which is not helpful. A softer alternative would be *"What was the thinking behind that?"* This will get you the same information without the defensive behaviour that may have accompanied it before.

Leading Questions

The good listener rarely uses leading questions as these are really designed to ensure that someone agrees with your point of view.

E.g. When faced with the question *"You think it's a good idea don't you?"* it is very hard to say no. If you really want to know what someone thinks ask them an open question: *"What do you think about this idea?"*

Hypothetical Questions

Hypothetical questions can have a really important role in the Leader's repertoire. These are questions which allow the respondent to consider an approach to a situation in a non-threatening way. They are especially useful in recruitment interviews when you are exploring issues outside the respondent's current expertise. Hypothetical questions are often phrased *"What if?"*.

E.g. *"If you were leading this team, what would you do to motivate people?"*

Probing Questions

Probing is useful when someone is giving you incomplete information or when you think that perhaps the issue has not been thought through. They allow the respondent to consider their options more fully without you having to give advice.

E.g. *"What do you think would happen if…?"*

"Can you tell me more about…?"

"What are the potential repercussions of taking that action?"

Reflecting Questions

Reflecting is useful when someone is giving you incomplete information or when it would be useful for them to think more deeply about the situation. The technique is simply to reflect what has been said to you, but as a question.

E.g. *"Do you understand that?"*

"I understand most of it"

"Most of it?"

Multiple Questions

There is a danger of asking several questions at the same time. When you ask an open question – wait for the answer. Often there will be silence as the person thinks about their response. Avoid being tempted to fill the silence as it will almost always be with a closed question. The respondent will answer the closed question as it easier to answer than an open question requiring more thought.

E.g. *"What do you think about that?"* silence. . . *"are you ok with it?"*

"Yes"

Summary

Effective questioning is crucial to eliciting accurate information. There are different types of question to elicit certain types of information. The key to getting it right is to decide what specific information you need first, **then** choose the best question to ask.

CHAPTER

13

Giving and Receiving Feedback...

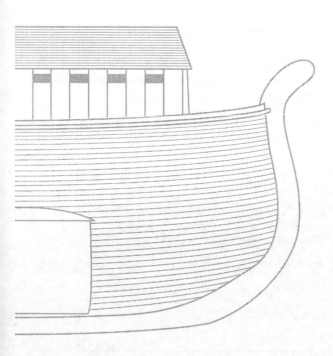

Giving and Receiving Feedback _____

This is another key skill for the Project Leader. We don't believe that anyone consciously decides to behave in a way that causes problems in a team; but people's behaviour can sometimes affect the project performance or outcome either in a positive or a negative way.

As Project Leader you need to be able to give feedback in a way that either modifies or reinforces a team member's behaviour.

The Process

Stage 1: Check your intention. Is it 'win-win'? I.e. will the recipient get as much benefit from the feedback as you? – if not, don't give any feedback

Stage 2: Always ask permission: e.g. *"May I give you some feedback?"*

Stage 3: Wait for the answer. Good teams have a contract where the answer is always "Yes" as they are aware of the value of feedback.

Stage 4: Give the feedback in this way:

1. *"When I see you..."*

   "When I hear you say..."

2. *"I think..."*

3. *"I feel..."*

Stage 5: Wait for the reply. The recipient says, *"thank you"* because they have been given valuable information. This is also the opportunity for the recipient to respond with any mitigating circumstances.

Stage 6: Give a recommendation as to how the recipient can change their behaviour or attitude to the benefit of all concerned.

"I recommend that you... stop/start/continue"

Stage 7: Choice: The recipient can now choose whether to accept or reject your feedback. Under this contract they cannot reject outright. They do, however, have the option to reflect. They must tell you which option they intend to take and must come back to you within 24 hours if they wish to renew this option e.g:

"I accept your feedback and as a result I will..........."

"I reject your feedback and thank you for the information"*

"I would like more time to reflect and will come back to you in 24hrs"

This process can be used for any form of feedback.

For example, someone who is consistently late for meetings, or someone who has dealt sensitively and effectively with a stakeholder.

*"When I **saw** you arrive late for meetings every day this week, I **thought** you were not interested in this project and I **felt** disappointed"*

"I'm sorry I was late, my Father is ill and I have to wait for the nurse to arrive every morning before I can leave him"

This response may cause you to change your initial recommendation from *"I recommend you start arriving on time"* to, *"I recommend that you start talking to me about anything that affects your performance on this project, because I wouldn't have thought and felt what I did if you had"*.

This reinforces the need to have prepared your recommendations before you start, but be able to respond once you have heard the other person's view.

Or:

*"When I **heard** you deal sensitively with that stakeholder on the phone I **thought** you clearly understood their problem and I **felt** really pleased. I **recommend** that you carry on behaving in exactly that way"*.

Giving, and receiving feedback can be difficult, especially if it is responding to problematic behaviour, but failing to give feedback gives the person no opportunity to change or reinforce their behaviour and may well cause you problems as the leader further down the line.

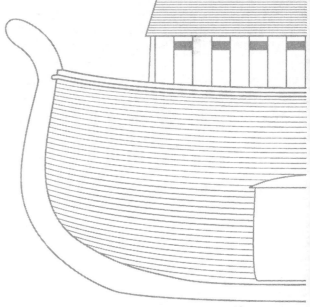

CHAPTER

Active Listening...

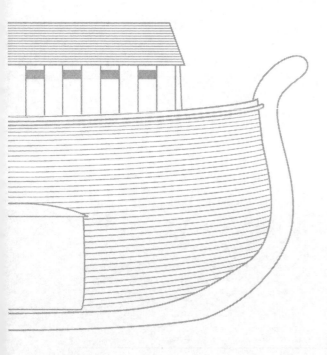

Active Listening

Many people believe that listening is something we do automatically; unless we are hearing impaired we each spend a large part of the working day listening to other people talk. However, if we were to ask those same people whether they feel truly listened to they may give a different answer.

People who do not feel listened to are less likely to contribute their ideas to a project team. Consequently, you may miss some really good creative ideas and potential problems.

Effective Project Leadership succeeds or fails on the ability to communicate effectively and a key part of communication is the understanding of the message you are receiving from your team members and other stakeholders.

Active listening is not just something we do automatically but is a skill that can be learned.

A good listener will be aware of the speaker's:

- Choice of words
- Tone of voice
- Body language

A good listener will:

- Work hard to build rapport
- Take the necessary time to listen
- Employ a range of questioning techniques
- Genuinely try to understand
- Use appropriate non-verbal behaviour
- Paraphrase regularly
- Demonstrate understanding
- Use eye contact effectively

In general we want more from a listener than just their physical presence. How many times have you tried to talk to someone who is quite simply more involved with their computer screen than they are with you?

Call to mind someone who doesn't listen to you, think about what you dislike about his or her behaviour and make sure that you don't do it yourself.

Words

Listen carefully to what the other person is saying; don't jump to conclusions before they have finished talking. The choice of words will also give you some indication of how strongly he or she feels about the subject matter.

Tone of Voice

Tune in to the tone of voice you are hearing, it will help you to pick up on the emotional content of the message. The person opposite you may be telling you that he/she is quite happy to work late on the project but the tone of voice could be telling you something else. Reflect this back to them and check out if your suspicions are right.

E.g. You are telling me that you don't mind working late tonight but you sound quite angry. Is that how you feel?

Body Language

Observing a person's body language can give us clues to how a person is feeling and can show us evidence of an imbalance between their words and their meaning. However, the observation of body language is not an exact science and you should always be cautious about diagnosing.

When we are listening to someone it is important that we don't get so focussed on his / her body language that we forget about our own. If you sit or stand in a relaxed position, with your shoulders and body turned towards the other person and with your arms relaxed by your sides you are conveying to that person that you are open to what they have to say.

Once you have established a good base for discussion you can focus even further on body language. As we have already discussed, matching a person's body language can help you to build rapport with them and can also give you some insight into how they are feeling. Try slouching down in your chair with your arms folded. How do you feel? Now sit up straight, relax your arms and smile. Do you feel better? If the person opposite you is slouched down how might he / she be feeling?

Eye Contact

Good eye contact is an essential part of active listening. Focussing your eyes on another person's shows that you are giving them your undivided attention. However, unbroken, staring eye contact can be threatening and invasive. Good eye contact will be broken regularly by flicking the focus away from and back to your colleague.

Paraphrasing and Summarising

Summarising is a very useful technique to demonstrate that you are really listening. It involves repeating back to a person a précis of what they have just said. It can be done at the end of a conversation or at intervals throughout the discourse to recap over what has been said to date. Summarising is also useful for checking that both parties are clear about what has been agreed or about any goals that may have been set.

E.g. *"So we're both clear about why this problem occurred and now we have discussed 3 possible ways of dealing with it. I am going to go away and look at the cost of replacement or repair of the machinery, you are going to consider whether better training might have prevented the problem in the first place and Eric is going to talk to the Plymouth depot to see if they have ever encountered this situation. Then we will all meet again on Wednesday to discuss progress."*

Paraphrasing is another useful tool for active listeners to employ. Similar to Summarising it also involves repeating back to a person a précis of what they have just said. The difference is that you use your own words, rather than the words of the person you are listening to. Regular paraphrasing can show that you are listening and that you have heard what you are being told. It also allows you to check your understanding of a situation.

E.g. **Mary:** *"My car has broken down and I am struggling with bus times at the moment. I have to get my son to school for 8.45 and then get the bus to work but the next bus isn't until 9 a.m. and it doesn't get here until 20 past at the earliest and it's been late every day this week and so have I."*

Edward: *"So you're finding it very difficult to get to work on time at the moment."*

You will notice that, in the example, Edward didn't try to solve the problem for Mary; he just showed that he understood what the problem was.

Above all active listening is not simply about listening but about demonstrating that we are listening. As a technique, it also helps you to remember what is said and reduces the need for you to take extensive notes – which can also break rapport with the speaker as it appears you are not listening.

Motivation and Delegation...

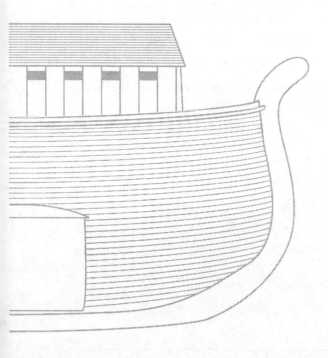

Motivation and Delegation _____

We have already seen that, as the Project Leader, your job is to ensure that the task is completed – not to complete it yourself.

Motivating the team, getting the best out of them is a key skill.

Motivation is either intrinsic (internally motivated) or extrinsic (externally motivated).

As the Leader, you can sometimes have some control over extrinsic factors such as reward, recognition and punishment, but it takes some effort to affect individuals' intrinsic motivation.

The challenge is to find out what motivates your team members: what aspirations, needs and wants do they have, and how can you meet those needs. This means that you have to talk to them and actively listen to their replies.

In terms of reward, you may not have any influence over financial elements, but you may be able to take the team for a drink, or give them some small but meaningful gifts – We know of one Project Leader who buys small trophies in the shape of milestones every time the project is on target. It may sound silly and trivial but the team members really value them – and work hard to achieve their milestones as a result. Celebrate success with the team.

Giving feedback to individuals and thanking them for their efforts really helps individual's intrinsic motivation. People generally respond well to being thanked and it's not something we do often enough. A response we often get is *"but we pay them for doing their job"*. That's right, but how much more does it cost to say thanks and show your appreciation for them helping you do your job?

There are lots of theories around motivation, and fundamentally people need to feel valued, and believe that they are adding value to be motivated to perform to their best. As the Leader, you can influence both of these factors.

What is delegation?

Delegation occurs when the Project Leader gives a Team Member the authority to take decisions within defined areas of responsibility.

Delegation saves you time and develops your people!!

The Benefits of Delegation

- Releases large blocks of your time
- Develops subordinates
- Improves motivation
- Creates time for planning and creative work
- Increases job satisfaction
- Inspires confidence and trust
- Quicker action
- Assessment of potential
- Aids succession planning
- Fosters teamwork
- Fresh viewpoint of task
- Platform for better work
- Creates opportunity for achievement
- Improved communication through feedback
- Reduce costs
- Improves all-round effectiveness

The Risks of Delegation

- Choose the wrong person
- Where to stop
- Halo effect
- Resentment from other staff
- Cost
- Mistakes
- Individual becomes overworked – stress
- Too many leaders

The Process of Delegation

Decide what to delegate

It is important to choose the tasks carefully. Don't just 'dump' something you don't like doing on to someone else.

Don't choose an activity which only happens rarely and will take longer to train someone how to do it than do it yourself.

Decide who to delegate to

Choose someone who will benefit from the development, and avoid using the 'willing horses' who will always take on something without complaint and become overloaded.

Interview to assess willingness

Very important. Ensure that you only delegate tasks to people who are really happy to take them on.

Additional responsibility and Authority needed

Do they need any additional formal authority or responsibility? Ensure that this happens, and that everyone who needs to know about this change is informed.

Provide resource

Do they need any physical resources? Room, IT equipment etc. Do they need extra time?

Additional training and experience needed (dates)

Organise any necessary skills training.

Decide target date for full acceptance

This needs to go on to your project plan.

Monitor progress

Give support and recognition

CHAPTER

16

Team Building...

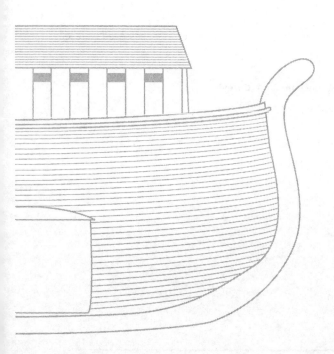

Team Building

It is often written that *"a team is a group of people with a common goal".*

This definition is somewhat simplistic though; a group can have a common goal and yet not necessarily be a team.

A successful team must have a common goal or a shared **purpose** and teams should regularly review the question *"what are we trying to achieve – and how are we trying to achieve it?"*

High performing teams also thrive in a climate where every individual is valued for the role they play within the team and therefore gains a sense of **belonging** to the team.

Finally, when a team becomes settled, its members can see everything that they hold in common and this helps them to form an **identity.**

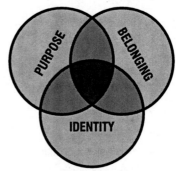

What stage is the team at?

When a group of people come together to form a team, it takes a while for them to settle to the task.

BW Tuckman described four distinct stages that groups experience as they develop into an effective team.

Unfortunately, there is no guarantee that all groups will naturally pass through each stage. The development of the team requires effort by the leader and the team members. The progression of the team can be gauged by observing their behaviour.

Stage 1. Forming (Testing)

- Polite
- Impersonal
- Guarded
- Watchful
- Concern for Structure
- Silence
- Anxiety
- Dependence

Stage 2. Storming (In-Fighting)

- Confrontation
- Opting out
- Sub-Grouping
- Conflicts
- Feeling stuck
- Noisy
- Rebellion

Stage 3. Norming (Getting Organised)

- Clear roles emerging
- Developing skills
- Establishing procedures and norms
- Giving feedback
- Confronting issues
- More open exchange
- Much/better listening
- Moving to group cohesion

Stage 4. Performing (Mature Rapport)

- Resourceful
- Energy task related
- Openness and trust
- Effective
- Close and supportive
- Settled Dependence

As the Leader, you have a responsibility to help the team move through each stage. By creating an environment of openness and honesty, with mutual trust and understanding and acceptance of difference you will facilitate the team moving through the stages quickly – this is often crucial for a relatively short term project team.

Remember the Project Leadership checklist on page 64? This will really help you to create and maintain the environment you need to ensure the success for your project, and the motivation of your team.

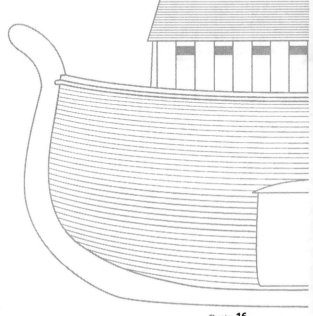

CHAPTER

17

Putting it into Practice...

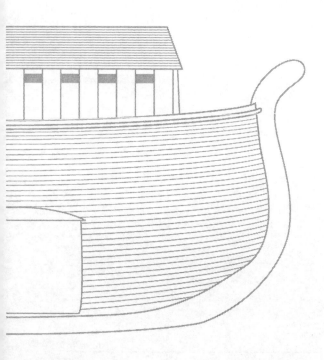

Putting it into practice _____

In this Chapter we explore how to facilitate the process as a project team leader and introduce you to some activities we have found to be really beneficial.

Fundamentally, this is a simple process – but not necessarily an easy one.

The key to making this process work effectively is how you facilitate each step.

Create an environment where everyone feels comfortable to contribute. Time spent on this stage is well rewarded later. Remember to focus on the individuals in the team and meeting the team's needs as a whole.

Use a light, airy and quiet environment, provide plenty of liquids and fruit to help the team members think and ensure that you have plenty of breaks.

It is crucial that everyone's contribution is noted and valued, otherwise they will stop contributing.

Discovery

Logical Levels

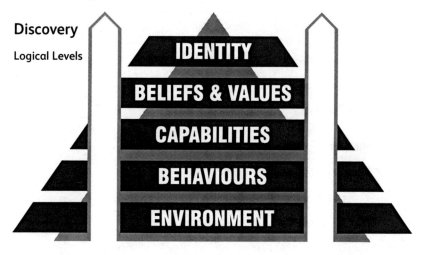

Generally: Facilitate discussions around each of the levels and capture the information on a sheet of headed flipchart paper.

If the team is a large one, split them into two or more teams of no more than 6 people and compile the results from the teams.

During this process, you will be starting at environment and working up through Identity to Purpose and collecting information about each step. At that point you will have a good understanding of where the team is at the start of the process. Following this, you will work back down the pyramid to environment.

Key questions for :

Environment

"How would you describe the project environment at present?"

"How else would you describe the project environment at present?"

"What is the geographical environment we operate in at the moment?"

"What is the physical environment?"

"How does it feel in this environment?"

Behaviour

"How do we behave in this environment at present?"

"What do we currently do in this environment at present?"

"How do we behave as a team at present?"

Capabilities

"What capabilities do we have at present to complete this project?"

"What helpful resources do we have at present?"

"What skills do we have as a team at present?"

Beliefs and Values

"What do we believe about this project?"

"What do we believe about this team?"

"What is important to us about this project?"

"What is important to us about how we complete this project?"

Identity

Use a series of random photographs and ask each individual *"which photograph represents the identity of the team at the moment?"*

Ask each individual to explain the reason for choosing that particular photograph.

Keep the chosen photographs as a record of the team's view of present identity.

Purpose

"Using the information gathered in Environment, Behaviour, Capability, Beliefs and Values and Identity, what is the Purpose of this team?"

Having captured the information relating to 'now' the next step is to take this purpose and apply it to the rest of the Logical Levels.

This process will identify the culture of the project team for the duration of the project.

Key questions are:

Identity

Given that the Purpose of the team is to. . . which photographs represent the team identity for the future?

Ask each individual to explain the reason for choosing that particular photograph.

Keep the chosen photographs as a record of the team's view of the future identity.

Beliefs and Values

"Given that the purpose of the team is to . . . what beliefs and values will we need to complete the project?"

Capabilities

"Given that the purpose of the team is to. . . what capabilities do we need to complete the project? What resources and skills do we need?"

Environment

"Given that the purpose of the team is to. . . what does the environment need to look, sound and feel like for us to complete the task?"

Review the final flipcharts and collate the information. A good way to do this is to photograph the flipcharts and produce a document of the photos.

This approach helps to 'anchor' the experience. When team members see the photos, they automatically remember the conversations and discussions that led to the ideas written on the flipchart. This doesn't happen if you just type up the content (it takes less time too).

How Did We Complete The Project To Write This Book?

Logical Levels

Environment now

- Matthew in Cheshire

- Martin Cornwall

- Matthew working in project environment – felt frustrated and restricted

- Martin training and facilitating plus coaching – feels fulfilled but more potential to develop

Behaviour now

- Matthew working in pharmaceutical companies trying to introduce learning from NLP course and applying it to projects. Also writing project management newsletter and working with an industry group writing a guide to project management

- Martin training NLP – developing applications for NLP tools and techniques

- Facilitating strategic planning for a range of organisations using these tools. Also writing about NLP on the blog

Capabilities now

CAPABILITIES — NOW
- EXPERIENCED IN THE FIELD
- DEVELOPED A NEW APPROACH
- BOTH EXPERIENCED WRITERS
- OPEN TO CHANGE (INC TECHNOLOGY)
- LIKE TRYING NEW THINGS OUT
- GOOD COMMUNICATORS

- Experienced in the field
- Developed a new approach
- Both experienced writers
- Open to change (inc technology)
- Like trying things out
- Good communicators

Beliefs and Values now

BELIEFS/VALUES — NOW
- IT WILL REALLY HELP PEOPLE LEADING PROJECTS
- THIS IS A BETTER WAY
  WE CAN WRITE A BOOK TOGETHER
- AUTHENTICITY, COLLABORATION,
- WALKING THE TALK AND MAKING A DIFFERENCE ARE IMPORTANT

- It will really help people leading projects
- This is a better way
- We can write a book together
- Authenticity, collaboration, walking the talk and making a difference are important

Identity Now

Images shown for demonstration purposes only. Please select your own. Images sourced from www.focusmm.co.uk

> PURPOSE
>
> ▷ TO START A REVOLUTION
>   IN THE WAY PEOPLE
>   THINK AND FEEL ABOUT
>   PROJECTS AND THE WAY
>   THEY BEHAVE DURING THEM

Purpose

- To start a revolution in the way people think and feel about projects and the way they behave during them

Identity - Future

Images shown for demonstration purposes only. Please select your own.
Images sourced from www.focusmm.co.uk

The Project Future

> BELIEFS /VALUES — FUTURE
>
> ▷ THERE IS A VITAL MESSAGE
>   IN THE BOOK
> ▷ IT WILL BE THE SPARK THAT
>   STARTS A REVOLUTION
> ▷ WE CAN DO IT
> ▷ IT'S IMPORTANT TO GET IT RIGHT

Beliefs/Values future

- There is a vital message in the book

- It will be the spark that starts a revolution

- We can do it

- It's important to get it right

Capabilities future

- We're good at hitting deadlines and milestones

- Use skype to avoid geographic problem

- Use google docs to avoid geographic problem

- We have a network to help us with design, publishing and book review

Behaviours future

- Getting on with it!

- Writing and feeling more energised with a sense of purpose

- Planning beyond the book

Environment future

- Partnership

- Trust

- Energy

- Geographical problem solving

Well Formed Outcome

Generally: facilitate the process and capture the answers to each question.

Do this as a full team, rather than splitting into smaller groups as it is important to reach a consensus at each stage.

What is the Goal? What do we want to achieve?

Be specific, state the goal as a positive. When you have defined the goal, use those words for the rest of the process rather than 'this goal'.

Where are we now?

Define the current position of the project against the desired outcome.

How will we know when we get there?

What will we see when we have achieved the goal, what will we hear (ourselves saying, other people saying, what sounds will we hear from the project?) and how will we feel when we have achieved the goal.

The language of the questions is important – presuppose that you will achieve the goal so use the word 'when' rather than 'if'.

Is there any other evidence?

To show that we have achieved our goal? This allows for any evidence that has not been covered by the last question. Sometimes the unconscious retains some key information – for this process to be most effective it is important to uncover as much information as possible.

What will this goal get for us? or allow us to do?

Ask *"what else?"* several times – you will find that the initial information is less important and valuable than subsequent information. A little like peeling through the layers of an onion, the later information is more motivating and important to the individuals than the earlier information.

Are we in control of achieving this goal?

It is very difficult to achieve a goal that you have no control over, if you find that you don't have control over the goal, there may well be some re-negotiation with the stake holders required.

When do we want to achieve this goal?

Set a date and a time – this may be influenced by stakeholders but as a project team you need to be in control so take control of your own deadline.

Where do we want to achieve this goal?

Is there any geographical context for the goal? There may not be so if that is the case, don't use this question.

Who do we want to achieve this goal with?

Again, there may not be a personnel context for the goal, so don't use this question.

What resources do we need to achieve the goal?

Explore the requirements for the project. List what you have already and what you need to have- time, money, people, equipment, skills and expertise.

What we will gain and what will we lose when we achieve this goal?

Explore the benefits for the stakeholders of the project, and look at any problems this project may cause as a result of achieving it.

Collect all this information – photograph the flipcharts again and create a document which then becomes the definitive goal of the project.

Our Well Formed Outcome For This Book

What is the Goal? What do we want to achieve?

We want to write and publish a book that collates all of our ideas about Project leadership

Where are we now?

We've got the ideas and we've developed and applied a process. We're enthusiastic and we haven't started writing yet.

How will we know when we get there?

We will see the book and see it posted on Amazon. We will hear pages being turned, gasps of surprise and people saying *"if only we'd read this years ago!"* we will be saying to ourselves *"we're published authors"* and we will feel fantastic.

Is there any other evidence?

People will be talking to us about using the book and we will be being asked to go and help people with their projects.

What will this goal get for us? or allow us to do?

It will help us to help people run much better projects. It will allow us to have fun in our work, it will allow us to work together and earn money.

We will feel a sense of satisfaction. It will change the project delivery paradigm and allow us to explore what's next.

Are we in control of achieving this goal?

Absolutely!

When do we want to achieve this goal?

30th September 2011 – we want to pre launch the book at the NLP at Work Conference.

30th October 2011 – produce 1st edition after review

What resources do we need to achieve the goal?

Knowledge – how to publish a book. We know a publisher to ask.

We need to create time to meet and write the content.

We need money to invest in the enabling structure.

What we will gain and what will we lose when we achieve this goal?

We will gain reputation, satisfaction and an altered sense of purpose.

We will lose time for other things, a sense of frustration that there is a better way of doing things and a feeling of being a lone voice in the wilderness.

Defining the Plan

It is much easier to look back to the past than to imagine the future. This is because it has already happened and we are much happier remembering something that has happened than imagining something that hasn't.

If you take a moment to remember the steps you took in your life to get to where you are today, you will probably be able to develop a list of those steps fairly easily.

If you imagine standing at the bottom of a mountain and looking up at the path you have to climb, you will be able to create a feeling that this will be difficult. It is often hard to motivate yourself at the bottom of a mountain, knowing the effort it is going to take to climb it.

If, on the other hand, you imagine standing at the top of that mountain looking back at the path you took to get to the top, the feeling will be different, probably an element of achievement – possibly tinged with relief?

The key to planning with this process is to imagine that you have already achieved the goal - you are standing at the top of your mountain, looking down.

We tend to think of, and represent time in our minds, as a line; with the future at one end of the line and the past at the other.

Try closing your eyes and thinking about the future. Imagine that you could point to your future; that your future is in a direction relative to yourself, perhaps in front of you, or to one side. Point to your future and notice what direction that is.

Now do the same for your past and notice what direction that is relative to you.

If you joined the two together you would have your timeline.

Planning

Generally, work in one group for this process. Set up a sheet of paper at one end of the room with the completion date written on it.

At the other end of the room, set up a sheet of paper with the real date on it.

You now have a timeline with the future and the present on it. Between the two you are going to put all of the project activities.

Take the team to the 'future' end of the room.

Explain that for this process to work, we need to pretend that we are in the future, at a point where we have completed the project and achieved the goals.

Explain that we are going to review the project and look at all the steps we took to achieve the goals.

It is really important that everyone uses past tense language for this process. Phrases like *"we need to. . ."* or *"we would have to. . ."* are not allowed and phrases like *"remember when we. . ."* or *"we communicated the project goals to. . ."* are important.

The reason for this is that is very easy to see the steps we have to take as a team, and it is also easy to get bogged down in detail, to see the problems that will need to be overcome and get demotivated.

By pretending that we have already achieved the goal, any problems have already been overcome and so we don't need to focus on the negative.

People might struggle with this thought experiment initially, but if you persevere as the facilitator, and correct any wrong tenses you will find that people soon start to behave as if this process is a review of the project, rather than a planning session.

Start a free flowing ideas session with everyone contributing to listing 'what we did'.

The best way to do this is to have a large stack of paper and give everyone flipchart pens to write their ideas with.

Keep this process going until you have captured everything.

Typically, there will be initial flow of ideas which will slow after a few minutes. There are a few ways to help people through this 'dead zone'.

1   Re-state the ideas already written – this helps to stimulate creativity.

2   Ask for 'one more idea' from everybody.

3   Ask *"what else did we do?"* several times – this implies that there are some ideas missing and people will search their unconscious to find the missing ideas.

The next step is to lay all of the sheets of paper on the floor in a line – this is the critical path. Ask *"what has to happen before each step?"* so that a logical order is created. There may be parallel activities so you may end up with more than one line.

Once the final order of activities is defined, the final step is to put dates to each activity. These dates will mostly be end dates, although some may be start dates for ongoing activities. The order for the sheets may change as you go through this process.

At the end of this process – you have a plan with milestones and end dates.

Each activity will probably be a sub-project in itself so you may decide to go through this process with some or all of the steps you have identified, but at this stage you have a complete top level project plan.

Thank the team and celebrate in some small but meaningful way.

TIMELINE

How to Build an Ark Project Timeline

30th October 2011 First edition published
15th October 2011 Peer review
30th September 2011 Book launch at NLP at Work conference
31st August 2011 Book complete - designed and proof read
31st July 2011 Final Draft complete
1st July 2011 First Draft complete
June 2011 Section: What if?
June 2011 Section: How?
May 2011 Section: What?
April 2011 Section: Why us? Why Now?
March 2011 Section: Why project leadership?

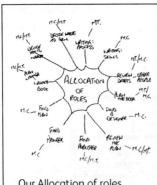

Our Allocation of roles
for the book project

Allocate Roles

This is a team activity. Use a flipchart and write the project title in the centre. Radiating out from the centre, list all the key activities. Ask the group to discuss the allocation of roles.

The purpose of this is to allow the team to allocate themselves to roles – if these are the best fit, they will be more motivated to fulfil those roles effectively than if the roles had been allocated to them.

See who volunteers for roles and how appropriate they are to fill those roles.

Make the final decision on who will be filling each of the roles and explain your reasons for choosing them.

If the previous stages of the process have been completed effectively, you will have little or no need to change the roles the group have allocated themselves. Be aware that some people may be overloaded because they have either volunteered (or been volunteered by the group) for too many tasks.

Delivery

Essentially, the delivery phase of the process is when you apply your leadership skills introduced in Chapter 10 to ensure that the team keep to the plan and the Project is completed effectively.

Evaluation

This is a team activity and is ideally facilitated by someone who has not been involved in the project, either as a team member, leader or stake holder.

The activity can be carried out as a single group or as a number of smaller groups depending on the size of the project team.

Essentially, the team needs to answer 5 questions:

1 What did we get right?

2 What did we get wrong?

3 What would we do differently next time?

4 What can we take from this experience to other projects?

5 What difference did we make?

We haven't undertaken this activity yet because we haven't completed the project – at the time of writing, the book hadn't been published.

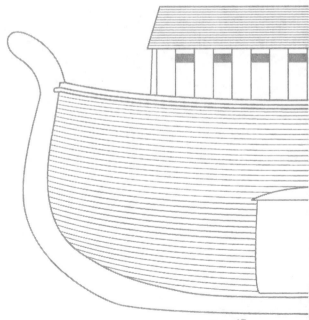

CHAPTER

18

Triage...

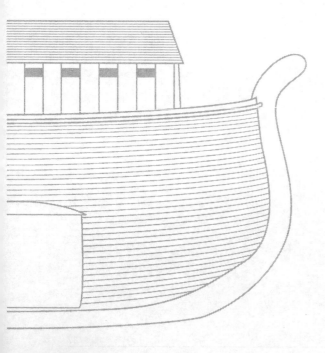

Triage _____

Is there a feeling that your project could be running better, does it look like it has a life of its own?

We've put together a check-list of some of the common symptoms that have come up for teams that we've worked with. You may have a problem that's not included. If that's true, rather than going through the check-list on page 118, it may be better to answer the four questions below.

To regain a sense of control over those things that you have influence upon, it helps to take bite sized pieces of the pie, to understand where you are and what you can do about it. There are several fundamental questions to ask;

How are you out of control?

This will enable you to pinpoint what it is that has given rise to the symptoms you experienced.

What needs to be controlled?

Identifies the parts of your project that you feel should be under control.

How are you going to take control?

Articulates the actions that you will take to move away from feeling like you're on a roller-coaster, towards a sense of being on top of things.

Where is the project, right now?

Provides the signpost towards the part of this book that describes tools or skills and their use for the stage your project is at. You may find for example that, although your project is in the delivery phase, it is more appropriate to step to an earlier phase, based on the actions you want to take. That's fine - projects evolve throughout their lives, and can benefit from revisiting earlier phases when changes or surprises happen.

These questions are even more powerful when you ask the team.

Triage Check-list

Do you recognise any of these symptoms, do some of them feel about right for your project, can you hear similarities with the situation that you're in at the moment?

Feels like you're running out of time ☐

Sounds like the money jar is nearly empty ☐

Are you missing the target for quality standards ☐

Does it look like you can't get out of the planning stage ☐

You don't know why you're doing this project ☐

You don't know what to do, the plan isn't clear ☐

Is the money being spent too quickly ☐

Does the team have different pictures of the project end point ☐

Are you moving on to the next stage of your project without checking it makes sense ☐

People aren't talking ☐

Lots of changes of people working in the team ☐

Does it feel like you're making the same mistakes ☐

Has the team "rushed into doing" ☐

Project roles or responsibilities are unclear, do others have a different view of them ☐

Spending more time fighting fires than planting trees ☐

If you have recognised even one of these symptoms, you're not alone. They're all expressions of the feeling of being out of control.

Here are our suggestions to address the symptoms you've ticked

Symptom	What can I do?
Feels like you're running out of time	<ul><li>Re-plan. How is your Well Formed Outcome different, what has changed?</li><li>Negotiate more time for the activities in question</li><li>Negotiate activities with the team to do what's needed in the time available.</li></ul>
Sounds like the money jar is nearly empty	<ul><li>Find out if the sounds you're hearing paint the correct picture</li><li>Negotiate additional resources</li><li>Negotiate an alternative delivery strategy</li></ul>
Are you missing the target for quality standards	<ul><li>Review the quality standard - is it too high or too low, then negotiate a change to the quality standard</li><li>Re-plan what is needed to achieve the target quality standard</li></ul>
Does it look like you can't get out of the planning stage	<ul><li>Look at your Well Formed Outcome, does this still make sense to everyone</li><li>Negotiate what else is needed to finish planning</li></ul>
You don't know why you're doing this project	<ul><li>Look at your project end-point, what is it about this that you're not clear of?</li><li>Negotiate a change to the end-point or objectives</li></ul>
You don't know what to do, the plan isn't clear	<ul><li>Review your project plan</li><li>Pin-point what it is that isn't clear, work with the team to find some clarity</li></ul>
Is the money being spent too quickly	<ul><li>Understand what "too quickly" means for you</li><li>Find out if what you're sensing is valid</li><li>Negotiate additional resources</li><li>Negotiate an alternative delivery strategy</li></ul>

Symptoms	What can I do?
Does the team have different pictures of the project end point	• Explore, together, your end-points, to create a clear, shared project end point
Are you moving on to the next stage of your project without checking it makes sense	• Look at the review points/milestones, what is happening or not happening so that the check isn't done • Negotiate adherence to your team's process for moving from stage to stage • Re-plan to reflect changes in understanding or information needed to take these decisions
People aren't talking	• Talk with people to understand what's happening for them • Who isn't talking, what leads you to think that they're not talking • Look for indicators of representational systems in use, does your communication fit with what you see?
Lots of changes of people working in the team	• Negotiate team stability with the resource holders • Re-plan to take account of the impacts of these changes
Does it feel like you're making the same mistakes	• Look at what is happening, where/who could give guidance • Re-visit Delivery tools and actions

Symptoms	What can I do?
Has the team "rushed into doing"	• Negotiate clear, shared end-points with the team • Check commitments
Project roles or responsibilities are unclear, do others have a different view of them	• Revisit your planning in Delivery - are roles agreed and unambiguous • Negotiate with team / leaders to get to clarity
Spending more time fighting fires than planting trees	• Check your decision points - are they in the right places • Look at what is happening, or not happening, that leads to fighting fires • Re-visit Delivery tools and actions

What's next?

You may wish to talk with Martin or Matthew about how to build your Ark. They can both be reached at Ark Project Leadership by phone, email, or on-line;

On-line: www.arkpl.com

Email: martin@arkpl.com
matthew@arkpl.com

Phone: 0845 415 4197

A final word

It is no accident that you picked up this book. At some point, you must have asked yourself, *"What can I do to make my projects less difficult to manage?"*. You took the time to explore the principles in this book that make the Ark project leadership approach such a successful way to make this shift. You may now think that Ark reflects a more empowering, rewarding and ultimately more effective way to deliver projects.

You may have already begun to think about ways in which you can extract ideas from this book and apply them to your own business or life experience. You may even have thought about how you can gain buy-in from other leaders in your organisation, so that you are truly equipped to ride the crest of the wave that is the post-industrial project. You might have thought about instilling organisational guidelines that embody the processes we've talked about. Guidelines that give people a picture of what it would look like to work together like this, giving them a sense of a different way of doing things.

Often, we get inspired by the ideas or practices of others, but we fail to put those ideas into operation. As you read this book, you may be feeling that you want to learn more about the key skills that Martin and Matthew have shared throughout this book.

Whilst you have been reading, you may have tried out several of the tools and processes that we've discussed, Perhaps you are thinking that you would like some reassurance, support and guidance as you take your first steps into this new world of project leadership.

You may have already tried some of the things in this book and been stunned by how successful they can be, how big the difference is that they make. You may want to be a part of the revolution. Please send us your stories so that we can share your success with people at the start of their own Ark building journey.

What does the future hold for you and your organisation? Where might the ark of project leadership take you? We suspect that it may be a journey into the extraordinary.

We enjoyed seeing the discussions that led to us seeing this book come alive. We hope you enjoyed reading it and will continue to enjoy using the processes in your projects.

Martin and Matthew July 2011

Lightning Source UK Ltd.
Milton Keynes UK
UKOW030705160413

209263UK00001B/15/P